Tomás Rivera

1935-1984

The Man and His Work

Bilingual Press/Editorial Bilingüe

General Editor
   Gary D. Keller

Managing Editor
   Karen S. Van Hooft

Senior Editor
   Mary M. Keller

Assistant Editor
   Linda St. George Thurston

Editorial Consultants
   Randall G. Keller
   John M. Ryan
   Juliette L. Spence

Address:

Bilingual Review/Press
Hispanic Research Center
Arizona State University
Tempe, Arizona 85287

(602) 965-3867

Tomás Rivera

1935-1984
The Man and His Work

edited by
Vernon E. Lattin
Rolando Hinojosa
Gary D. Keller

Bilingual Review/Press
TEMPE, ARIZONA

ISBN: 0-916950-89-1

Library of Congress Catalog Card Number: 88-71440

PRINTED IN THE UNITED STATES OF AMERICA

Cover design by Christopher J. Bidlack
Cover illustration by José Antonio Burciaga

Acknowledgments

The editors wish to thank the following for permission to print or reprint material appearing in this volume:

Concepción Rivera, for:
    Always and Other Poems, which was first published by Sisterdale Press (Sisterdale, TX) in 1973.
    "The Searchers," which first appeared in *Ethnic Literatures Since 1776: The Many Voices of America.* Eds. Wolodymyr T. Zyla and Wendell M. Aycock. Lubbock, TX: Texas Tech Press, 1976, 27-31.
    "Poetics."
    "Chicano Literature: The Establishment of Community," which was first published in *A Decade of Chicano Literature (1970-79)*, eds. Luis Leal, et al. Santa Barbara, CA: Ed. La Causa, 1982.
    "Richard Rodríguez' *Hunger of Memory* as Humanistic Antithesis," which was first published posthumously in *MELUS*, 11, 4 (Winter 1984): 5-13.
    "The Role of the Chicano Academic and the Chicano Non-Academic Community," paper presented at UT Austin Invitational Symposium, Hispanics in Higher Education: Leadership and Vision for the Next Twenty-Five Years, April 29-May 1, 1982.
    Inauguration Speech, University of California, Riverside, April 28, 1980.
    Commencement Speech, University of California, Riverside, 1980.
    Letters to Luis Leal (17 nov. 1963 and 9 June 1976), Américo Paredes (23 mayo 1978), Rolando Hinojosa (10 Oct. 1978), and the Hispanic community (April 1980).
    Statement of Personal Outlook on the Future of American Higher Education.
    Curriculum Vita.

Armando Martínez-S. and the Tomás Rivera Archive, University of California, Riverside, for:
    Photographs appearing in the inserts between pages 6 and 7 and between 152 and 153.
    Section IV, In Memoriam: facsimile letters from the Regents of the University of California, Rafael J. Magallán, Rubén S. Ayala, Esteban E. Torres, and Lloyd Bentsen.
    Children's poems by Richard Guel and Paul Silva.

American Association for Higher Education, One Dupont Circle, Washington, D.C., for the three Tomás Rivera Lectures by John David Maguire, Alfredo G. de los Santos, Jr., and W. Ann Reynolds.
José Antonio Burciaga, for his suite of drawings in the insert between pages 70 and 71.
Luis Leal, for his article, "Remembering Tomás Rivera."
Sooner Magazine, University of Oklahoma, for James H. Abbott, "Tomás Rivera: So Proud of You Forever," in Vol. 4.4 (Summer 1984): 21-23.
Pat Mora and Arte Público Press, for "Tomás Rivera," which first appeared in her book *Borders* (Houston: Arte Público Press, 1986).
Héctor P. Márquez, for "Corrido de Tomás Rivera."
José Villarino, for "Homenaje a Tomás Rivera."
All the other authors who contributed original articles or poems to this volume.

TABLE OF CONTENTS

V. Poetry in Memory of Tomás Rivera

Children's Poems

Corridos and Other Poems

VI. Essays and Lectures for Tomás Rivera

VII. The Archive

VIII. The Last Song

[*Insert: Photos of Tomás Rivera*]

IX. Bibliography

PREFACE

In 1977 I knew Tomás Rivera only as a name. I had read his novel, ". . . *y no se lo tragó la tierra,*" and I had talked about his work and his career with friends who knew him. On a cold winter day, after talking to Rolando Hinojosa about a keynote speaker for the First Midwest Latino Conference on Higher Education, I called Tomás and invited him to be that speaker. Rolando's suggestion was the right one and Tomás Rivera accepted the invitation to come to Northern Illinois University that February. Why did he come to the frozen corn fields of Dekalb, Illinois?

He came because he knew the Midwest as a migrant worker.

He came because he knew that Chicanos and Hispanics lived and worked throughout the United States.

He came because he wanted to reach out to Chicanos and contribute to their life.

He came because he knew that the human voice, the personal contact, was magic.

He came because he knew the power of words and of communication, and he knew that an individual can make a difference.

We are all better because Tomás came to DeKalb, and because he contributed so much. That night in February he spoke to a crowded room of Hispanics from throughout the Midwest. Most of them will not today remember much about his presentation on Mexican immigration, but they will remember Tomás. I remember Tomás. That first impression, reinforced many times in the years to come, was of a strong but gentle man who loved life and loved people. During the years to follow, his face and spirit seemed not to change at all. He remained as I remember him that first night I met him.

This volume in honor of Tomás is a small contribution, a small repayment, for all that Tomás gave us. It is perhaps fitting that Rolando Hinojosa is a co-editor. He was responsible for my meeting Tomás in February 1977.

All of the contributors to this special volume of *homenaje* to Tomás Rivera have their own memories of Tomás. Each has been touched by his life and his works in different ways, yet each remembers. Their contributions to this volume are their way of honoring that memory and that man, Tomás Rivera.

VERNON E. LATTIN
UNIVERSITY OF WISCONSIN

I. Introduction

Section II, Works by Tomás Rivera, contains poetry, articles, letters, and statements written by Tomás during the course of his life and made available to the editors of this volume through the Tomás Rivera Archive at the University of California at Riverside, and with the permission of his wife, Concepción. Long out of print, reproduced here is his 1973 collection of poetry, *Always and Other Poems*, as well as the more recent and better-known "The Searchers," which inspired John David Maguire's address, contained in section VI of this volume. Also contained here are statements by Tomás on his sense of poetics and his personal outlook on the future of American higher education. In addition, we have published three important essays by Tomás (on Chicano literature, the role of the Chicano academic and the Chicano non-academic community, and certain problems related to Richard Rodríguez's *Hunger of Memory*), as well as his 1980 inauguration speech upon being invested as chancellor of the University of California at Riverside. Finally, a number of facsimile letters are reproduced here, ranging in time from a 1963 letter in which he relates to Luis Leal, who was to become his close friend and mentor, a passion for the study of *literatura hispanoamericana* to a 1980 letter expressing his hopes for quality education for the Hispanic community.

Section III, The Professional Life of Tomás Rivera, contains his *vita*, an account of his professional life which we don't believe has been published before. The *vita* is followed by a biographical review by Rolando Hinojosa. Few people were closer to Tomás as a writer and man than Rolando. The two sides, professional and human, should be seen together and Rolando gives us both. Perhaps this account of his life will inspire someone to begin a much needed biography. It should be noted that as this book goes to press, it has been announced that the Tomás Rivera Archive has been awarded a grant to complete a documentary film about the private and professional life of Tomás.

Following Section III is a series of drawings by the noted Chicano artist, José Antonio Burciaga. This suite of renderings expresses the artist's multifaceted emotions and perspectives on Don Tomás.

Section IV, In Memoriam, contains a facsimile of the memorial tribute of the Regents of the University of California as well as a representation of facsimile letters honoring his memory. Also reproduced here is a tribute from his dissertation advisor at the University of Oklahoma, James H. Abbott, as well as remembrances by Luis Leal, Alfonso Rodríguez, and Ron Arias. Arias, a fellow Chicano novelist, writes a letter to Tomás. Ron's memory and those of Rodríguez and Leal again are about the professional and the human, with the stress on the personal. Tomás gave us both literature and himself, and Arias reminds us that it is Tomás's life, "Yours was the best story of all," that we treasure most. Arias's willingness to share with us his letter to the dead Tomás attests to his depth of feeling. He reminds us that Rivera left us with a vacuum that cannot be filled, but that he also left us Pete Fonseca and other characters whom we can experience again and again. Similarly, Luis Leal highlights the creative work of Tomás Rivera, including the second novel he was working on, *La casa grande*.

Alfonso Rodríguez's essay is about his memories of Tomás and about how Tomás took his own life and turned it into fiction. Rodríguez, formerly an eighth-grade general science student in Tomás Rivera's classroom and currently a Chicano poet and a professor of Hispanic Studies at the University of Northern Colorado, thus combines fact and fiction, memory and imagination, to recreate for us a portrait of Tomás Rivera and his literature. His essay, "Tomás Rivera: The Creation of the Chicano Experience in Fiction," informs us that fiction grows out of lived experience and that the experience of fiction is also an historical event. As he writes, "*Tierra* is the radiography of a people. The Chicano experience, in real life and in the novel, is universal."

Dr. Rodríguez's experience with Tomás Rivera began in 1954 when his family moved from Mexico to Crystal City and took up residence at 307 Valverde Street near the Rivera household. Whether this was destiny, an act of Providence, or happy accident, it placed Rodríguez in a unique location at an important historical time. Alfonso was to grow up as a close friend of Tomás's brother, Tony, and to live through the political changes in Crystal City that were the paradigms for the Chicano movement.

Thus Dr. Rodríguez sees the first framework story in *Tierra*, "El año perdido," as an allegory of the Chicano people in Crystal City around 1963. Trapped like the boy-hero in a cycle of unawareness, frustration, and impotence, the Chicanos are awakened by the voice of their collective unconscious, and they break the cycle of oppression. For Rodríguez this is a fiction, a history of the city, and a personal reality. Thus the particular historical experience reveals the universal.

Rodríguez's essay presents much that is important about Tomás Rivera's life, the experience of the Chicanos in Crystal City, and of the novel *Tierra*. His fusion of memory, history, and fiction is testimony to Rivera's novel and suggests an important way of rereading the novel. By returning to the historical space and time of growing up in Crystal City, Texas, with Tomás Rivera, Rodríguez recreates both that reality and the fiction that grew out of it. Those of us who were not there share the experience and, by sharing that history, we can re-experience the fiction. Fiction is not life, but the interplay of the two in the lives of both Rivera and Rodríguez forces us to think more carefully about the relationship to the two "realities."

Section V, Poetry in Memory of Tomás Rivera, presents poetry written by nine adult and two child poets who seek to remind us of Tomás Rivera and the Chicano experience he so magnificently portrayed. Some of the poets were close friends of Rivera, familiar for years with his life and his work. Others knew Rivera only through his literature and yet were deeply affected by this paper knowledge. Both groups of poets, those who knew him in life and those who knew him in writing only, reflect deeply on what his existence meant. They all see a man and through that man the Chicano and the human experience.

Poets like Galván, Alurista, Rodríguez, and others in this volume were close personal friends of Tomás Rivera and their poetry reveals a sense of both the personal and literary loss in Tomás's death. Alurista's poem, "bartolo's kuilmas," like so much in this volume, combines the literary life and the personal existence, the Bartolo of fiction and the real city, the poet of *Tierra* and the poet of this earth. Alurista's haunting and powerful poem forces us to remember, to remember the smile and the struggle, the sweat and the sweetness. It is what Tomás Rivera's literature forced us also to remember.

Other poems, like those of Pat Mora and Irene Blea, remind us primarily of Tomás Rivera the man. They tell us of how we were honored by the man and of what we have lost. They tell us of a life lived and given to the Chicano people. They reflect on the roots of his life and the fruits that he left us, of "the boy from Crystal City, Texas/not a legend to be shelved/but a man whose *abrazos* still warm/us. . . ."

Other poets in this volume, like Paul Trujillo, did not know Rivera personally and they seek to honor Rivera the artist. Having just completed a reading of Rivera's *Tierra*, Trujillo writes his poem, "A Child was Born." As Trujillo says in a letter accompanying the poem: "The stories (from *Tierra*) read like memories I had long forgotten. They evoke tears, a sense of spiritual wonder. Although I know next to nothing of his life, I feel as if I know his spirit. In a way it strikes me as specifically Chicano. But, like a tree (with roots in a particular culture), the branches and the leaves open into the sky of humanity.'' Thus Tomás reaches out after death to others, to new readers.

Section VI collects the three distinguished lectures given in honor of Tomás Rivera at the national conference of the American Association of Higher Education. Tomás Rivera was a member of the AAHE's Board of Directors and an active member of the association. This is the first national organization to honor Rivera with an annual memorial lecture and this event attests to their sense of value and to the influence that Tomás Rivera had on higher education in this country. Often we are so caught up with Tomás Rivera the man and the artist that we forget the professor and administrator, the lecturer and the Chancellor. These lectures remind us of all of these components and are valuable contributions to the honor of Rivera and his lasting influence.

The first lecture in March of 1985 was presented by John David Maguire, president of Claremont University Center and Graduate School. Those of us who heard the lecture were impressed by the power of the words and the emotion and strength of the delivery. At the beginning of his lecture, Maguire speaks of Rivera's prophecy and says, ''The question is whether we can make good its promises. This talk is a call for us to render real in the public world those commitments that constituted this good man's life and were his search.'' Maguire's commitment to what Rivera stood for is evident not only in the lecture, but in the fact that shortly thereafter he opened at Claremont the Tomás Rivera Center, a center for policy analysis. For those who did not hear the lecture we urge you to read it carefully and to remember its closing remarks: ''Tomás was an old vision for whose realization we still must seek, an old dream searching to become young again. Tomás Rivera was our sorrow for mankind's inhumanity. He is our pledge to make it whole.''

Alfredo G. de los Santos, Jr., Vice Chancellor for Educational Development, Maricopa County Community College, the second distinguished lecturer in this series, reaffirms the pledge that Maguire spoke about in the first lecture, and reminds us that all people and all countries are interrelated and interdependent. His speech on Mexican America is thus a speech about all of the global realities. His concern about the education of Chicanos in Mexican America is a concern about all people who are not allowed a proper beginning. He says, ''How Hispanic youngsters do in school is important to the future of higher education but also to the future retirees—to the future of American society.'' Unfortunately, the all-too-familiar statistics that he presents show us how poorly Hispanic youths are doing in education. The gap in educational attainment between Chicanos and whites is critical and it raises a question that must be asked over and over again: ''Are we headed for a bimodal society with one group educated, white, affluent, older and retired and the other group uneducated, minority, poor, and young?'' Alfredo de los Santos is unwilling to accept the ''yes'' answer to this question, and his lecture concludes with suggestions about how educational policies can be modified to change the face of the educational reality for Chicano children. Tomás Rivera, an educator, would have sat in the audience listening to Alfredo and nodding in agreement.

W. Ann Reynolds, Chancellor of The California State University, delivered the 1987 Tomás Rivera lecture at the National Conference of the American Association for Higher Education. She informs us that within a month of her coming to California, Tomás

> journeyed to my office to welcome me, with that gentlemanly chivalry he possessed. He was the only higher education leader in the state to do so, incidentally. After a warm welcome, within fifteen minutes he had enlisted me in an organization he had founded to promote

greater involvement of minorities in higher education. Tomás, consider that you enlisted me for life—you started the warmest and most worthwhile call to service of my professional lifetime.

Dr. Reynolds, with the help of her colleagues in the California State University system such as Tomás Arciniega, President at the California State University at Bakersfield, and chair of the Commission on Hispanic Underrepresentation, continues to work toward increasing the number of Hispanics in the constituent colleges of the system, even as it is the largest single educator of Hispanics in the nation.

The last two essays in this section are new contributions to the scholarly writing on Rivera's novel, "*. . . y no se lo tragó la tierra*," and on his other works. It is as an artist and novelist that we most fully remember Tomás Rivera. He first gained national attention through *Tierra* and in rereading the novel we continue to know more about him. We are especially glad to present in this volume these two important contributions to the growing critical bibliography about Rivera.

Santiago Daydí-Tolson's article is an extended study of ritual and religion in Rivera's writings. This study interrelates the works of Rivera with the intellectual development of the Chicano consciousness and worldview. Teresa Rodríguez limits her study to Rivera's novel and to some of the techniques of the art. Taken together the two essays present some new and important critical views, adding to the growing awareness of Rivera as artist.

Section VII presents information about the recently established Tomás Rivera Archive at the University of California at Riverside. Armando Martínez-Standifird, the archivist, who has been extremely helpful in identifying valuable material for this *homenaje*, describes the holdings and future plans of the Tomás Rivera Archive.

Section VIII is a brief conclusion in which there is really no concluding. This volume is testimony to the endurance of Tomás Rivera in so many lives, in so many written words. Alurista's poem, "it has been said that when/the poet misplaces sorrow/his song is lost," repeats a truth about poets and about Tomás, who never misplaced emotions.

Finally, Section IX is an updated bibliography of writings about Tomás Rivera and his works.

VERNON E. LATTIN
UNIVERSITY OF WISCONSIN

ROLANDO HINOJOSA
UNIVERSITY OF TEXAS, AUSTIN

GARY D. KELLER
ARIZONA STATE UNIVERSITY

Tomás Rivera's high school graduation picture, Crystal City High School, Crystal City, Texas, 1954.

Tomás Rivera (left) and Jacinto Quirarte at the University of Texas at San Antonio, c. 1973, discussing the artwork for the latter's book *Mexican American Artist* (Austin Press, 1973).

Photo taken to illustrate the "Interview With Tomás Rivera: A Chicano Writer," by Elsa Nava, at UT San Antonio on April 11, 1974. Photograph by Marta Alvardo. "I didn't see myself as being poor. But I saw other people as being very poor, and yet we were living in the same conditions . . ."

"To me fiction is an exercise in inventing. It's not my intention to moralize . . . Let the readers themselves do the moralizing." From the interview with Elsa Nava (April 11, 1974); photo by Marta Alvardo in Rivera's office at UT San Antonio.

Photo of Tomás Rivera while he was Associate Dean of the College of Multidisciplinary Studies at the University of Texas at San Antonio, c. 1975.

"Literary" pose (c. 1976) taken while Tomás Rivera was at UT San Antonio to promote his novel and short stories.

Left to right: Angela de Hoyos, Tomás Rivera, and Margarita Cota-Cárdenas at Floricanto Tres, Third National Chicano Literature Festival, June 14-19, 1976, San Antonio, Texas. Photo by Moses Sandoval.

Tomás Rivera while he was Executive Vice President and Acting Vice President for Academic Affairs at the University of Texas at El Paso, c. 1978.

II. *Works by Tomás Rivera*

ALWAYS AND OTHER POEMS

Seeds
in the hour of seeds

Dawn light
Fractured by profiles
Touches of life breathing

Anticipated death
prevails
in exhaling essence
Dawn light
separating your profile

The seed,
mine,
yours,
is here, alive
We
One

Have we liberated light?

Full . . . now
Profiles . . .
You triumph
as light
totally prevails

You,
our son, and me
isolated by light

You,
our son,
seeds we are
in prime light
in dawn light
in the hour of seeds

Past possessions

A piece of string
A broken top
A crooked kite
A wooden gun
A mop . . .

Quiet . . . noise

A long thin weed a lance
A few large cans a dance
   Boxes
For cars and houses

Such trivial things

Young voices

Young voices,
fresh,
loved by the wind
Grasped,
Delighted,
Held by the wind

New voices
young voices
who soften the wind
eternally loved
carved forever
into the wind

In the night
the wind is a lover
of young voices
of love seeds
scattered
pollen
eternal

For the voice
is the love seed
in the dark

Perfection of perfections

Hands entwined
through arms and waists

perfection of perfections
the young bodies

Beauty,
no more beauty than this
there is

in the night
in the night
in the night

to never wait for the light
to savor love
the crystalization of their beauty

Do they know?

Yes

Always

You have seen yourself
for you have been looking
out the door

Always

You never sleep
          never dream
You wait for yourself

Always

You have seen yourself
You were here before
many
yesterday
today
ever
behind the door

Always

Another me

There must be
There has to be
another me

For how would I know,
why would I want to know?

There must be
There has to be
another me

Our children,
am I in them or
they in me?

I was the leaf
That I know

This solitude

solitude, dark, blackness
through powers of the body
grasping of me
puzzlement
through eyes
unwanting

grasping tightly
images of despair
bits of light, rays
contemplation of sorrows

dull upon dullness
sitting on every dream
so distant now
so distant
so damning to this life
to this darkness
to this solitude
to this dark
       waning
           nodding
               smile

Run, Puff, run, run

We look and see
We come and go

An arm, legs, a head
to be filled
to be filled

Not to think
Not to love
Not to move

To be filled
To be filled

not to be

Jump, jump

Run, Puff, run, run

The overalls

Frightening
as the attic hole
the overalls in the garage, hanging
and the vapor from the train
swung to my face
as the cross that
shouted the lump
in the cemetery
and the sounds of clods
of earth hitting the coffin
reminded me of something
I knew nothing about
the glancing of tearful eyes
embracing
as I sensed
that I had been born
the crushing vapor
and the overalls, hanging
in the garage
never to be filled again

A most tired word

Love
a most tired word
replacement needed
overused
abused
love
a most tired word
beyond hollowness
seeking itself
it is

Soundless words

Words without sound
how terribly deaf

What if I were to remain
here
in the words
forever?

Ennui

desk	pencil	voices
people	words	faces
cars	windows	clothes
paper	war	children
towns	houses	cities
nations	presidents	laws
joy	death	sorrow
religion		
man		
stars		
dirt		
flowers		
animals		
birth		

world
worlds

Autumn and Winter

The wind
The beauty
The cold air

humbles the people

The sun
The leaves
The broken twigs

they bow their humility

Reminders

to bend the head
in chest, and
to suck in a
death-smelling air
while the wind and cold
circle the sun

One last gaze at the warm beauty

THE SEARCHERS

I

How long
how long
have we been searchers?

We have been
behind the door
Always
behind screens and eyes
of other eyes
We longed to search
Always
longed to search

"naranja dulce
limón partido
dame un abrazo
que yo te pido"

We searched through
our own voices
and through
our own minds
We sought with our words

A la víbora, víbora
de la mar
de la mar
por aquí pueden pasar

How those words
lighted our eyes
From within came
the passions to create
of every clod and stone
a new life
a new dream
each day
In these very things
we searched
as we crumbled
dust, our very own
imaginary beings

Hey, ese vato, chíngate

A terrón lighted our eyes
and we watered it and made
mud-clay
to create others in

II

The search begun
so many years ago only
to feel the loneliness
of centuries
Hollow—soundless centuries
without earth

How can we be alone
How can we be alone
if we are so close to the earth?

Tierra eres
Tierra serás
Tierra te volverás

Una noche caminando
una sombra negra vi
Yo me separaba de ella
y ella se acercaba a mí.

¿Qué anda haciendo caballero?
¿Qué anda haciendo por aquí?
Ando en busca de mi esposa
que se separó de mí.

Su esposa ya no está aquí,
su esposa ya se murió
Cuatro candeleros blancos
son los que alumbran allí.

III

Death
We searched in Death
We contemplated the original
and searched
and savored it
only to find profound

beckoning
A source that continued the search
beyond creation and death
The mystery
The mystery of our eyes
The eyes we have as
spiritual reflection
and we found we were
not alone

In our solitude
we found our very being
We moved into each other's
almost carefully, deliberately

Had we been here before?
What do we have you and I?
Only our touch, our feeling
shared, that is all that we have
life in such ways, way
again, again, again
We found ourselves in ourselves
and while touching
we found other mysteries
that lay beneath
every layer of truth
unwinding each finding
another lonely vigil
another want, desire
to find
to find what?

What we always had?
Did anyone know that we
were searching?
That every look toward the earth
was a penetrating search that
had lasted for years
the mystery of time halted
and unknown without
itself discovery

IV

At night we searched each other
Somewhere was the soul
Somewhere in there was the heart
Somewhere in the night

was the lonely eye of the soul
Motionless
Waiting

Sometimes we found it
and slept with our lips
on it till the light fractured
everything

Can we find something every day
and every night?
We believed
yes, we had been finding
for centuries

Other beings?
We,
one,
the very same flavor
the very same
We looked behind heads
at the back of heads
The back of white heads
was less dangerous
Sometimes we turned the
heads around only to find
eyes that didn't see
who dared not see
who dared not be
without our own

No estamos solos.

V

We are not alone
if we remember and
recollect our passions
through the years
the giving of hands and backs
"dale los hombros a tus hijos"
We are not alone
Our eyes still meet with the passion
of continuity and prophecy

We are not alone
when we were whipped
in school for losing
the place in the book
or for speaking Spanish
on the school grounds
or
when Chona,
dear Chona,
a mythic Chicana,
died in the sugar beet fields
with her eight month
child
buried deep within her
still
or
when that truck
filled with us
went off the mountain road
in Utah
with screams
eternally etched among
the mountain snows

We were not alone in death

VI

We were not alone in Iowa
When we slept in wet ditches
frightened by salamanders
at night
reclaiming their territory
and we
killing them
to maintain it as our—
then, our only—possession
or
in San Angelo
when we visited the desiccated
tubercular bodies of
aunts and uncles
friends and lovers

We were not alone
when we created children
and looked into their eyes
and searched for perfection

We were not alone
when taught
the magic of a smile, a kiss
an embrace each morning
and to feel the warmth
and quiver of a human
being

We were not alone
murmuring the novenas,
los rosarios, each night,
los rosarios we hoped
would bring joy and lasting peace
for Kilo
killed and buried in Italy in 1943
or
when we gathered each night
before bed
and waited
for the nightly sound
of the familiar cough
and the sweet/pan dulce
that it brought
Warm milk/pan dulce
opened the evening door
or
when we walked
all over Minnesota
looking for work
No one seemed to care
we did not expect them to care

VII

We were not alone
after many centuries
How could we be alone
We searched together
We were seekers
We are searchers
and we will continue
to search
because our eyes
still have
the passion of prophecy.

POETICS

Poetry is one of the most human of experiences because it begins with nothing. It is the birth and death of the word and the poet, as he freezes abstractions, severs relationships with his utterances. Poetry is finding the search, finding the word. It is not inventing, but finding, starting the invention. Yet, poetry should not be explained, categorized, studied, but read and felt and sung. Poetry denies the poet but not his expression, and utterance. Poetry, then, is a way of becoming nothing and everything. In a way poetry is and is not what Octavio Paz says—"knowledge, salvation, power, abandonment." Poetry gives me pure feelings—time, beauty, man, and original death.

CHICANO LITERATURE:
THE ESTABLISHMENT OF COMMUNITY

I took the idea for this study from a lecture by Robert Hine, a professor of history at our University of California at Riverside. During the spring of 1980, at the 29th Annual Faculty Research Lecture titled "Community, Utopia and The Frontier," he established the essence of community in the American West. As I listened to his presentation his ideas became very relevant to Chicano literature in the last ten years in a variety of ways. So I have titled this presentation "Chicano Literature, 1970-1979; The Establishment of Community."

In the last ten years Chicano literature has established community, myth and language. Or at a minimum, it has reflected the urge and desire to establish such elements by the Chicano ethnic group. The flourishment and the now documented last ten years of literary effort reveal these very attitudes, problems and the very exact efforts of the exteriorization and the imaginative and inventive efforts of the Chicano. The different genres extol also the most important literary characteristic, as it is in all literary, creative and essayistic enterprises, the struggle for intellectual emancipation. The Chicano community will never be the same again. It is a changing, dynamic community. We in the Chicano community realize this and we are also aware that the changes will be broader and faster in this decade. Chicano literature will reflect this as it has done for the past decade.

The anxiety to have a community, the urge to feel, sense and be part of a whole was the most constant preoccupation and need for Chicano students and faculty alike in academia in the past ten years. Surely this was also the case for the Chicano community outside the walls of academia (Or was it not? I do think we have to ask the question.) which was trying to form something out of a very diffused nation or a very diffused tribe. Chicano literature as it began to flourish in the 50s and 60s revealed a basic hunger for community (*hambre por una comunidad*). Here was a group of kindred people forming a nation of sorts, loosely connected politically and economically and educationally but with strong ties and affinities through its folklore and popular wisdom. Also there were ties through varying degrees of understanding of its historical precedence and a strong tie because of its language. Yet the political and social organizations of the Chicanos were weak within, and existed within sophisticated North American and Mexican societies that really had not cared about the development of the group itself. Clearly, the impetus to document and develop the Chicano community became the essential *raison d'etre* of the Chicano Movement itself and of the writers who tried to express that.

The different *planes* that were evolved called for the establishment and betterment of the Chicano community above all else. One of the most important goals was to establish a *lugar* or a place. Aztlán became the place in most writings. Myth or not, the urge to have, to establish and to nurture a place of origin, of residence became the most important need to meet. This was not surprising. This deep need for community revealed basically a colonized mind and a deprived, powerless class. The Chicano had to begin decolonizing the mind. The start, the beginning steps, were to declare a place of residence—to establish a community and to document that community. As Martin Buber has stated, "Community is the aspiration of all human history." And Chicanos were human, and Chicanos had a history. And very definitely, in the late 60s and early 70s, I believe that the Chicano community began to aspire very deeply for its sense of community.

I want to digress briefly to establish the idea of community in the United States and especially in the West. I am quoting and paraphrasing Robert Hine's effort in delineating community, Utopia, and the Frontier for American society as a whole. I want to take these concepts and apply them to Chicano Literature—the effort itself, its content and its form. Professor Hine states the following:

> In 1940, Wheatland, Missouri was probably as typical a small town as one could find. The citizens were well knit. They were asked if their pioneer ancestors were any more well-knit than they. The answer was yes. They were downgrading the present (1940s). Hundreds of others were saying that society was prevailingly alienated, fragmented, atomized; and they would look back at a pioneer past and say the past was better. Also, in the scholarly area, distinguished people like Yi Fu Tuan, in his work *Landscapes of Fear*, describes a type of innocent, fearless past which became alienated from its natural environment and sinks into an anxious present. Samuel B. Warner, Jr. finds that most people living in the modern world, particularly in the large urban settings, feel as if they are existing in a clearing in a vast wilderness—that wilderness is the city. The only thing that they can know is the small clearing. And this has happened, says Warner, because the city has chosen deliberately to ignore its goal of community in favor of other goals. And these other goals are competition and innovation. The citizens of Wheatland, Missouri and others in 1980 are examples of people who are thinking about what is known as modernization theory—a theory that says roughly that we are engaged in accelerated economic growth associated with a psychology of getting ahead, a psychology of production, and that this leads inexorably toward the destruction of community for American society as a whole. On the other hand, there are large numbers of scholars who are pointing over and over again at a very strong community in the modern world. Scott Greer, Robert Redfield and even Oscar Lewis find particularly among kinship groups in modern cities strong elements of community.

Now, what is community? According to Robert Hine, community is the following:

> All definitions of community argue that first of all, community is a place [*un lugar*], a geographical location where they know people, know that the sun will come out behind a particular place, the formation of clouds, the place may be architectural features, a barrio, a nick on a building, color, age, material things, all of which express continuity [*una continuación de las cosas y así del espíritu*]. Secondly, community is a set of personal relationships. These are usually related to the size of the community but the primary thing is the personal relationships that must be primary in a community. Rebecca West says that "the community is conversation." [*La comunidad es conversación; la comunidad es platicar*]. Thirdly, the community is values. The values of the group over the individual. These values say that the whole is more than the sum of each of its parts. As a community works out, as these elements come into play, there is a tension of individuals versus the group. There are the tensions of a family within a community. And within the family itself is the basic building block. The family is also different elements—class, hierarchy, and it is class and hierarchy which make for the strong building power in the community. The ideal community is one which can make all these factors work [*valores, conversación, lugar*].

If we take Professor Hine's definition and place it parallel to structures, plots, ethos, motivation, characterization, etc., of Chicano literature of the past ten years, there is an almost exact correspondence. Works such as *Bless Me, Ultima, Estampas del Valle*, ".... *y no se lo tragó la tierra*," *Revolt of the Cockroach People, The Road to Tamazunchale, El diablo en Texas, Peregrinos de Aztlán, Caras viejas y vino nuevo*, are explicit in their urge for community and as such they are moods of community. Likewise in many works of poetry and short fiction, the basic preoccupation is *el lugar, la comunidad*. If in Spanish, and to a lesser extent in Mexican literature, there has been a tendency for the action of the literary work to over-impose itself on the thematic underpinnings, I believe that in Chicano literature of the last ten years that the idea of community has imposed itself on the action and theme of literary works. (*Las ganas de tener comunidad han sido muy fuertes*.) I also believe that specifically in the theater this is the case. (*El pueblo se sobreimpone*.) Community was a major preoccupation for the literary festivals such as *Flor y Canto* and *Canto al Pueblo*. There was a constant preoccupation that the community partake as well as participate in the *certámenes*—fully involved in the presentations or in the audience.

The community is place, values, personal relationships and conversation. What better description than this is there to define a work by such a distinguished Chicano writer as Rolando Hinojosa-Smith in which we find *lugar, modales, relaciones personales, conversación* as constant motifs. I think that it was because of the strong urge to establish a community that Chicano literature imbued itself with the preoccupations and the notions of proficiency and didacticism, especially the latter. As part of that communal urge to establish residence was the strong desire to teach the people (*el pueblo*) in a meaningful manner through literary works while at the time to seem proficient to the total North American public.

In the last ten years in poetry, theatre and short fiction, and in the novels, I perceive an effort, at times overly obvious, to deal with the traditional beliefs, customs, sayings, constant allusions to the supernatural, legendary symbols. These are the elements of coherence of the Chicano community and the writer utilized these common denominators to give form to an amorphous group. The Chicano writer took on the responsibility to document and preserve what sometimes existed quite unreflectively among "la gente." The writer speaking from the community, through characterized members, thus extracted the wisdom, the advice, and counsel from the community. This has been considered by many critics as a flaw in Chicano writers. I do not think it is a flaw. I contend that the more definite and national the person is in a literary setting, the more universal the motivation and the more revealing he or she will be of original elements of human perceptions and motivations he or she possesses. In this manner both place and person exist as primary units that hold basic original elements of humankind, that is, the total crystalization of passions—love, hate, joy, *tristeza*, etc.

The following two short pieces are both by Rolando Hinojosa-Smith. These are written some eight years apart. They have a basic theme. They reflect not only an evolution but a difference in style and emphasis and sensitivity. The first is titled "La güera Fira" (English version: "Fira the Blond") and is found in *Estampas del Valle*, and the other is a poem titled "Old Friends" from *Korean Love Songs*.

Fira the Blond

Without beating around the bush: Fira the Blond is a whore: She doesn't pretend to be a whore (like maids do) nor does she whore around (like society women); no. Fira's a whore and that's that. There's more. Fira has blue eyes, short hair which she doesn't dye and a figure that would stop the hiccups of don Pedro Zamudio, the parish priest.

Fira isn't from around here. She's from Jonesville-on-the-River. The daughter of a Mexican woman from Jonesville and an Anglo soldier from Fort Jones: She wasn't the first to leave nor the last, but, truthfully, she certainly has to be the most beautiful woman of the Valley. (The person who really knows a lot more about the people of Jonesville is don Américo Paredes.)

Fira is a serious woman who carries her whoredom like school girls carry their books: naturally. After she bathes, she smells of soap and water and when she goes to work, the curls by her temples are still wet.

She works in the tavern owned by Félix Champión, an illegitimate son of my Uncle Andrés. She neither dances nor struts from table to table nor flirts nor carries on. Don Quixote used to say that being a go between was serious business; that may be, but the occupation of being a whore in a simple tavern of a one horse town is nothing to laugh about either.

The women of Klail know who she is and what she is and that's it. If they gossip, that's their business but the majority don't; the majority don't gossip. Women usually tend to be understanding when they feel like it.

The only bad part of it all is that Fira won't last much longer in Klail: It's too small and, to tell the truth, money's scarce around here.

I believe that the folkloric elements and the pueblo's way of expressing itself are clearly evident in the development of this unique character and that these are also present in a series of anecdotes throughout the *estampas*. Some eight years later Hinojosa writes "Old Friends," which deals with the same theme but from a much more personal and gentle perspective, written in English.

Old Friends

In Honshu, the bigger island,
The southern Japanese businessmen call their whorehouses
Emporiums. Off Baron Otsuki Boulevard,
In Southeast Kobe, are five emporia, all in a row.

The nominal owner of Shirley's Temple of Pleasure Emporium
Is middle-aged Tomiko Sambe.
She prefers to be called Shirley.
And when she says it, it doesn't sound anything like that.

(Here, on an earlier medical R&R
Tomiko replaced my lost dress Army shoes,
For a week or two, with black navy shoes of proper fit.)
My good acquaintance here, Mosako Fukuda,
Has a brother named Hideo who's a medical student in Nagoya.
Mosako, native to the Kobe-Kyoto-Osaka Triangle,
Visits her parents in Nara every ten days or oftener, and always
When the cycle comes and lays her low.
There's no pretense here:
Her parents know where she works,
And I, learning the ways of the world,
Do not add insult to their injury
By visiting their home. I know of them and of Hideo through her.
And, like the popular song now,
        'She's never been to Tokyo,
        Hokkaido is out of the question.
        She's been once to Kyushu, but never to Shikoku.'

She loves to walk, and she loves the parks.
We go and stay until the familiar shimbun!—enough—
Enough, she says, and we walk back to Shirley's.

And now, midday of the sixth day of R&R, and
Despite what Berman claimed,
The shoulder's stiffened up again, thus
Making this just one more of Mosako's love duties.
As she starts on the shoulder,
She hums and sighs, and
When she tickles *me, she* laughs. I laugh, too,
And after this, the usual bath and mat and bath again.
We're a likely pair, we are; and I'm certainly no Pinkerton

To her Butterfly, but I *have* come to say goodbye. Later tonight,
We'll go shopping and then I'll leave with nine days left on my R&R.

Early next morning,
The World War II vets sweep the Temple of Pleasure Emporium
While we enjoy a quiet breakfast of pastry and tea.
Tomiko, who prefers to be called Shirley,
Comes in and we shake hands, Western style. After her tea,
We take long, full bows just like the old friends that we are,
And Mosako will walk me to the K-K-O Railway less than three blocks away.
She holds my pass, my ticket, and the money;
She puts them in my pocket, in a flowered envelope, and then
I surprise her with yet another fan (which she needs like a hole),
But she takes it, and her eyes close when she smiles.
Then her eyes and mine open wide when the train surprises us, and we watch
The rushing crowds.
   Gently with her fan,
     She pushes me away, and
       again her eyes close
When she smiles. She turns,
Walks away, carefully opening and studiously closing the fan
As the train rears back before
Moving on. I look for a familiar patch or face,
And finding none,
I remove my cap in time to catch the last
Faint smell of the tea and pastry
Prepared by my old friend.

As we recall these two pieces, in "La güera Fira" we have examples of the type of cameos we find throughout *Estampas del Valle*. I believe Hinojosa, among other things, attempts to build a community by the development of so many of these characters. He creates a true community in *Estampas*, above all else. The language itself is the language of conversation. (Es una conversación con gusto.) The elements of the community and the acceptance by the community of la güera Fira as part of its existence are very exact. "La güera Fira" makes up part of the whole of which the group is made. She fits. The language is oral—descriptive and realistic.

In "Old Friends" we have an example of an impressionistic endeavor. Here we have the language and the sense of reflection. Also well-understood is the attitude of acceptance and thematic intent to reveal acceptance of relationships and mature perspectives of men and women. It is also a very subjective poem although it appears to be very realistic. It is not the building or re-building of a community. Although these two pieces are different there are elements, common denominators, that are part of both which have elements of folkloric intent. One is the concept of cohabitation (vivir y dejar vivir). That is, the acceptance in the community of all types of people without signaling out a pejorative or positive value as to the role of people in the community. There is no attempt to denigrate anyone because of the state or position in the community. There is the wisdom of acceptance and the wisdom of relationships between men and women no matter what their position, social class, rank or endeavor. And more specifically there is the respect for individual condition and situation. The folkloric elements of Chicano literature that were so apparent in the early part of the 70s still carry forth in several ways the wisdom of the Chicano community. I believe it is the folkloric and oral language that brings forth the wisdom of the people. Literature in this sense becomes the history of customs.

Perhaps the most important element of Chicano literature is that it was able to capture from the beginning of the decade this very wisdom of a very disparate and amorphous nation or kindred group. It was able to do that because there was hunger not only in the community but in the Chicano writer to create a community. Up to the present time, one of the most positive things that the Chicano writer and Chicano literature have conveyed to our people is the development of such a community. We have a community today (at least in literature) because of the urge that existed and because the writers actually created from a spiritual history, a community captured in words and in square objects we call books.

RICHARD RODRÍGUEZ'S *HUNGER OF MEMORY* AS
HUMANISTIC ANTITHESIS

Although I was born in Texas, had lived in many states in the Midwest and had not lived in any Spanish-speaking country until then, my public voice as well as my private voice was Spanish through my first eleven years. It was in the fifth grade, that *eureka*! to my surprise, I started speaking English without translating. I suppose that at that time I had two public voices as well as two private ones.

Hunger of Memory is an exceptionally well-written book. It is a profound book, a personal expression which one learns to respect for its sensibility. To respect this type of sensibility is something I learned in the Spanish-taught "escuelita," which I attended before entering public school at age seven. What Richard Rodríguez has written has great value. However, I have difficulties with concepts in the book which I consider anti-humanistic. For several reasons I consider *Hunger of Memory* as a humanistic antithesis. This book has been controversial for the Hispanic in general and in particular to the Mexican American or Chicano. This has been the case much more so, I think, because it seems to be so well-accepted by the North American public as a key to understanding the Mexican American and debates related to bilingual education and affirmative action. Thus, it is important to define and perceive the book from different vantage points. Hispanics, Chicanos and Latinos are not a homogenous group. They are as heterogenous a kindred group as any that exists in our present society. They are at different levels of development, perception, understanding and as complex and therefore as complete as other human beings. Richard Rodríguez's book is a personal expression, an autobiography, and it must be understood as that in its singularity. It should not be used as a single way or method of understanding the bilingual, bicultural phenomenon of the Hispanic group.

I do not know Richard Rodríguez. I have seen him on television. I have read *Hunger of Memory* three times. I intend to read it again for it has much to offer. The work becomes more with each reading.

Richard Rodríguez's essays have a style and tone which complement and establish his concepts. *Hunger of Memory* establishes its tone through patterns based on the ideas of silence and the centrality of language—silence versus non-silence, silence and active language, silence and culture, silence and intelligence. The aggregation of silence seems to indicate that if a person does not speak, he/she lacks intelligence. This is a view generally held by many teachers in the classroom: How can one judge silence? If a child's hand does not go up, if a question is not asked, the teacher's perception is usually that there is a lack of intelligence. Richard Rodríguez insists on the presence of his signal-silence and the public voice. If a person does not speak he/she does not have a public voice. How can one have a personal voice only in silence as the only true aggregate? The author indicates that Spanish was and is his personal voice. But it is an inactive passive voice that became neutered, sterile, and finally silent—dead.

I find underlined throughout the text a negation of what is fundamentally the central element of the human being—the cultural root, the native tongue. As one reads each essay, one progressively recognizes that what is most surprising for Richard Rodríguez is that silence and his basic culture are negative elements, regressive ones. This pattern of negation is softened somewhat when he thinks of his parents and his love for his parents, but he ultimately comes to the thesis that this silence and the consequentially inactive community is something regressive or negative. The dealing with silence reminds me of my efforts in struggling with this phenomenon of silence when I studied in Mexico and lived with Mexican families; especially in the rural communities, where I tried to write about what I considered the impenetrable face/masks and their silence. But I never thought for a moment that their masks did not conceal an imagination or thought processes, not that they were not developing and inventing constantly their own world view and perceptions. And that, although they were not speaking to me and hardly to each other, they were not actively thinking. Richard Rodríguez delves into silence, and writes from silence as he himself tells us, "I am here alone, writing, and what most moves me is the silence." Truly this is an active task for him. Yet, with regard to his own family, he sees this silence as a non-force. He finally concludes simplistically, unfortunately, that his personal voice is Spanish and that his active voice is English. Surely, this is a humanistic antithesis.

It is necessary at this point to call attention to his development as a writer. He grew up and was taught in the humanities. The humanities have a clear base — at a minimum the explaining or aiding in the elaboration of a philosophy of life. Surely by the time one is twelve years old or so one has a philosophy of life. By then one has formulated and asked all the great philosophical questions and has even provided some answers. Whether one asks and answers in English or Spanish or in any other tongue is not important. The humanities, and certainly the study of literature, recognize this. As an educated scholar in literature, certainly, and much more so as a Renaissance scholar, Richard Rodríguez should know this. But his thoughts do not recognize this fundamental philosophical base. Clearly as a youngster of twelve or thirteen years of age he could not have, but certainly as an academic he could have reflected on the realities of his life, on the sensibility, and on the importance of what he did not know then and what he must now know. The humanities are also, to put it simply, a search for life, a search for form, but most significantly a search for wisdom. In this regard Richard Rodríguez starts out well. His search for life and form in the literary form of autobiography has as a premise the basic core of family life. But then Richard Rodríguez struggles with the sense of disassociation from that basic culture. Clearly, he opts to disassociate, and, as a scholar, attempts to rationalize that only through disassociation from a native culture was he to gain and thus has gained the "others," that is, the "public" world. Without wisdom he almost forgets the original passions of human life. Is he well educated in literature? For literature above all gives and inculcates in the student and scholar the fundamental original elements of humanistic endeavor without regard to race or language, much less with regards to a public voice. The most important ideas that the study of the humanities relate are the fundamental elements and values of human beings, regardless of race and nationality. Ultimately, the study of the humanities teaches the idea that life is a relationship with the totality of people within its circumstance.

Then we come to the question of place and being. In Spanish there are two verbs meaning "to be," Ser and Estar. This is quite important to Hunger of Memory. Being born into a family is equal to being, Ser. Education and instruction teaches us to be, Estar. Both are fundamental verbs. Ser is an interior stage, and Estar is an exterior one. To leave the Ser only for the Estar is a grievous error. Richard Rodríguez implies, at times explicitly, that the authentic being is and can only be in the Estar (public voice) and only there is he/she complete. And further, he states that authenticity can only come by being an exterior being in English in the English speaking world. In the Hispanic world, the interior world of Ser is ultimately more important than the world of Estar. Honra, honesty, emanantes from and is important to the Ser. Richard Rodríguez opts for the Estar world as the more important and does not give due importance to the world of *Ser*. He has problems, in short, with the world from which he came. Surely this is an antithesis to a humanistic development.

As with memory, the centrality of language is a constant pattern in the book. For the Hispanic reader the struggle quickly becomes English versus Spanish. His parents do not know the grand development of the Spanish language and its importance beyond their immediate family. However, Richard Rodríguez should, as an educated person, recognize this grand development. Surely, he could have given credit to the development of a language that has existed over six hundred years, which has elaborated a world literature, which has mixed with the many languages of the American continents, which is perhaps the most analytical of the romance languages, and which will be of such importance in the twenty-first century. Instead Richard Rodríguez flees, as a young man, from this previous human achievement. This fleeing is understandable as a symbol of the pressures of the Americanization process. Yet, as a formally educated scholar, reflecting upon that flight, he does not dare to signal the importance that the language has. Instead he sees it as an activity that has no redeeming value. He gives no value to the Hispanic language, its culture, its arts. It is difficult to believe that as an educated humanist he doesn't recognize the most important element of Hispanic culture—the context of the development of the distinct religions in the Spanish peninsula—the Judaic, the Christian, and the Moorish. These distinct cultures reached their apogees and clearly influenced Spanish. As a humanist, surely he must know this. The Hispanic world has elaborated and developed much in the history of ideas. Richard Rodríguez seems to indicate that the personal Spanish voice lacks the intelligence and ability to communicate beyond the sensibilities of the personal interactions of personal family life. This is intolerable. Hispanic culture has an historical tradition of great intellectual development. He does not recognize the so-called "original sin" of the American continents. What is the *pecado original* that Hector Murena wrote about so eloquently? It is simply the act of transplanting the European cultures to the American continents. The conquest by the Europeans of what is today Hispanic America is one of the most fundamental struggles for justice. The Laws of Burgos (1511-1521), established in Spain before the conquest of Mexico, held above all that the Indian was a man of the world. This was a fundamental axiom. The evolved mestizo nations struggled through a racist colonial empire, but there was a mixture of races. This was less evident in the English speaking world. I mention this because it appears to me that one of the greatest preoccupations of Richard Rodríguez is that he "looks" Indian. He speaks of his father as looking and being white. He speaks of his mother as looking Portuguese. It surprises me that as an educated humanist in 1982 he would still have that type of complex, colonized mind. He feels out of place in Bel Air in L.A. because he looks Indian. He worries about what or how he will be perceived by the "Anglo." These are honest and sincere perceptions. I respect his feelings. He does, however, remind me of students I had in the 50s and 60s who were struggling with their brownness.

The Hispanic colonial period evolved a racism based mainly on color and, of course, class. The colonial mind was preoccupied with color. When a child born to a couple was darker than the parents, he/she was called a "*salto atrás*," a jump backwards, but if the child was lighter, he/she was considered a "*salto adelante*," a jump forward; and if the child was the same color as the parents, a "*tente en el aire*," suspended. At times Richard Rodríguez clearly illustrates a colonized mind. His reactions as a young child are understandable. As a writer, however, while interpreting these sensibilities well, he fails to analyze those pressures that force conformity and simply attributes negative values to the language and culture of his parents, who have, as he states, "no-public-voice."

It is well to recall briefly the formation of the Mexican nation and its history as it went from a political to an intellectual emancipation from 1811 to 1917. It took the Mexican nation over 100 years and 50 civil wars to evolve an independent, clear, and creative character. It is a unique nation. By 1930 the Mexican character was distinct—its art, music, literature, and culture were unique. It had developed a unique identity and character; it had accepted the mestizo. Surely, Richard Rodríguez must recognize, now that he is educated, that his parents came from a culture that was distinctly Mexican, and non-imitative, that his parents represent a culture with a singular identity. He offers, however, no recognition of the cultural uniqueness of his parents. Mexican culture had gone through its colonial and imitative period, its struggle for intellectual emancipation, and had arrived as an authentic, unique nation. His parents, therefore, recognize much better than Richard Rodríguez who the "gringos" are. This is a constant motif in the book. His parents know who they are themselves. They are no puzzle unto themselves. Richard Rodríguez says that change is a constant and should be constant and he argues that in order to change or to have the dynamics of change it is necessary to leave behind his Mexicanness, represented by the silence of the personal voice, the non-public voice, and his distinct cultural attributes. By gaining the other public voice, he asserts, he will become more authentic. Truly, this is antithetical to a humanistic education.

Richard Rodríguez's views remind me of two excellent books. The first one was published in 1930 by Samuel Ramos, *El perfil del hombre en la historia de México* (The Profile of Man in the History of Mexico), and the other was published in 1950 by Octavio Paz, *El laberinto de la soledad* (The Labyrinth of Solitude). *El perfil* discusses the inferiority complex of the Mexican. *El laberinto* reflects on the silence and the bursting out from that silence of the Mexican psyche. They are books eloquent in their perceptions of silence and the negativistic attitudes about the Mexican psyche. Samuel Ramos writes about *el pelado*; Octavio Paz has a marvelous chapter on *el pachuco* and now with Richard Rodríguez there is a total book on *el pocho* or what he considers to be *el pocho*. *El pelado, el pachuco* and *el pocho* can be considered alienated persons at the margins of culture. They do not represent the totality of the Hispanic culture in general, nor, in particular, the Mexican or Mexican-American culture. These are books about extreme people. What the *pelado*, the *pachuco*, and what Richard Rodríguez symbolize is a type of graffitti. By saying this, I do not seek to demean Richard Rodríguez's endeavor at all, but simply to point out that the most important element of graffitti is that it is an expression. Done in silence. Powerful. Exact. It calls out attention to itself as if saying "I want to understand myself," "I want you, the passerby, to understand me. I am at the (extreme) margin. I want to be; I hunger to be part of your memory." Graffiti beckons us. It calls to tell us that they *are* us—in an extreme way, that they exist between cultures, but outside a culture.

In spite of its humanistic antithesis, *Hunger of Memory* has an authentic dimension. Perhaps the most important element here is that Richard Rodríguez is a reflection of a North American education. Is he a reflection of the English professor or the place of preparation which doesn't really give him perceptions other than those of the English-speaking world? There is, ultimately, I believe, a lack of understanding of world culture; especially lacking is an understanding of the Hispanic world. It is a reflection of a North American education. He calls himself Caliban in "Mr. Secrets." Who is Caliban? He is a slave, a monster, a character in Shakespeare's last play. Caliban represents the puppet, the person who is controlled. Caliban in *The Tempest* was driven by material instincts only. "Mr. Secrets," the last chapter, is especially clear on this concept. Is Caliban a reflection of a North American education? Is it an indication of an education which refuses to acknowledge as important only that which is tied to the northern European cultures? Is it an attitude of non-inquiry in the teaching of humanities? Aren't racist impositions, Adamic and nativistic concepts and attitudes quite prevalent?

The great surprise of many of our students who study abroad is that of finding out that not everything is originated (truly) in the United States, and that in reality our cultural history is quite short and in many instances limited. Richard Rodríguez is saying that he now has a public voice, an authentic one. Before he did not. He now believes that he is more real, and this is absurd. The dimension that Richard Rodríguez gives the North American public in his book fits well within North American intellectual circles because he has ironically justified his context by "being" not one of "them," but rather by having become one of "us." The North American public accepts Richard Rodríguez quite well and much in the same manner that it accepted Oscar Lewis's studies of the poor in Puerto Rico and Mexico. In this manner, knowledge of the unknown is accepted, simplified, and categorized. One has to ask if Richard Rodríguez has a community now? Did he have a community in the past? Does he think that now because he has published and has been accepted as a good writer that he now has a community? Richard Rodríguez exists between two cultures, but he believes it more important to participate in one world than the other. But it is possible to participate in many worlds profoundly and without losing, but rather gaining, perception and appreciation from all.

I want to place in opposition to Richard Rodríguez's work a body of Chicano literature which has precepts as profound and as well written. This body of expression has not had the same acceptance. Some of it is written in Spanish, some in English, and some in a mixture of both languages. It is not recognized well, basically because the works have not been published or merchandized by major American publishing companies. In these Chicano works there is little hunger of memory, and much hunger for community. If Richard Rodríguez has hunger of memory, Chicano literature hungers for community. Those who labored, in the 1960s and 1970s and into the 1980s to establish a literature, accepted the task to develop a literature in the United States and that it was to be in languages understandable primarily to the Mexican-American community. The endeavor was a basic challenge to North American literary dominance. In 1965, there were few works written by writers of Mexican extraction in the United States. There were no courses being taught in Chicano literature. Today there are courses taught in Chicano literature in a total of 135 universities at the undergraduate and graduate levels. It is recognized as a body of literature either as part of Mexican literature, as part of American literature, or as an offshoot of Hispanic-American literature. It has several intellectual bases, but this literature does not interest Richard Rodríguez even as a curiosity—even though, paradoxically, he is now inextricably part of that contribution.

The Chicano writers I have in mind were hungry for community. The manner of establishing that community was through remembrance and rediscovery of commonalities of the culture plus the need to accept the community in all its heterogeneity—that is, with all its virtues, with all its flaws, with all its energy, with all its apathy. It was important to recognize and to develop the basic elements of our community. Martin Buber's idea that "Community is the aspiration of all human history" was clearly before us. The Mexican American as part of human history had to develop that community, to be part of it, or leave it. Rebecca West says that "Community is conversation," and the Mexican-American community has not been silent since then. What the Chicano writer did was establish a community where there was a definite place, where dialogues could develop, and where the values of the community could be elaborated. There was little concern regarding acceptance by the larger/majority population. There is a more visible Chicano/Mexicano-American community today because Chicano writers aided in underlining the realities that made up the community. Clearly Richard Rodríguez regards that community as living in silence. Actually that is why he is very alone. What one senses in *Hunger of Memory* is that his parents no longer speak. Ironically his parents speak louder than he. The sensibility of his writing effort, I dare say, does not come only from his training in the English language, but from those early day experiences when he was taught, I am sure, the way to invent himself in the world by his parents.

I said earlier that Richard Rodríguez reminds me of students I had in college in the 1960s who were embarrassed to organize themselves, who did not want to bring their parents to college to participate in college activities because their parents wouldn't know how to dress, and students who hardly respected the few Chicano professors who were then around. Truly, these students had the same type of colonized mind dramatized by Richard Rodríguez—honest, authentic, and naïve, particularly at this later date.

What *Hunger of Memory* therefore reveals is one more step in the intellectual emancipation of the Mexican American. It represents a significant intellectual step because such views are so clearly articulated. His parents know who they are, who they were, and who the gringos were. They didn't stop talking to him because they didn't understand him, but because he no longer saw the significance of their life. Richard Rodríguez lost the memory of all the philosophical questions they had helped him face and answer long before he walked into the English-speaking world. A writer is lonely only if he has lost the sense of his community's aspirations and the integrative values. His parents are the thesis of his statement. Sometimes, he feels frustrated because they have not read García-Márquez, Rubén Darío, but then he never read these writers to them. He hungers for a memory that could be so close, yet he doesn't seem to realize that satisfying this appetite is within reach.

Hunger of Memory is thus a humanistic antithesis for several reasons. First, because its breadth and dimension is so narrow, unaware as it is of the traditions that should inform it. Second, it is ultimately an aggregation of cultural negations. Richard Rodríguez prizes as authentic only that which he learns in the classrooms. Third, he underlines the silence of culture as negative. Finally, Richard Rodríguez believes that it is only through English that he thinks he can elaborate what is correct and not correct for the community as a whole.

In his last chapter, "Mr. Secrets," as the family is leaving, and everyone is standing outside, his mother asks him to take a sweater to his father because it is getting cold. The last words of the book are "I take it [the sweater] and place it on him. In that instant I feel the thinness of his arms. He turns. He asks if I am going home now, too. It is, I realize, the only thing he has said to me all evening."

Here Richard Rodríguez tells us that his father has been silent all evening. What he doesn't tell us is that he (Richard Rodríguez) has also been silent. He does not tell us about *his* own type of silence. If he has a hunger of memory it is mainly because he does not choose to communicate his more intimate memories. Can anything be that painful? Where is the real *honra*, the real *Ser*? The only positive cultural attributes which he signals throughout his book are those relative to the English-speaking world. Richard Rodríguez understands the needs for memory, but does not dare recover it totally. Why? The title is the thesis, but the content is the antithesis of the very title. This is a classic work, 1930 Mexican vintage, clearly seeking approbation of an inferiority complex. As Samuel Ramos stated in *El perfil del hombre*, it is not that the Mexican is inferior: it's that he thinks he is inferior. This was the legacy of Spanish colonization. Richard Rodríguez apparently decolonizes himself by seeking to free himself from a personal voice, but in so trying he will likely enter another colony of despair.

THE ROLE OF THE CHICANO ACADEMIC
AND THE CHICANO NON-ACADEMIC COMMUNITY

The relationship of the Chicano academic and the Chicano non-academic community is very important because of the cultural, political, social, economical and educational reasons. It is important for both beings.

What has been the role and contribution? One could say simply that the role and contribution has been for the most part through a model. What model? The answer is confused for there are several models, all of which can be judged as good and bad. One could also say that the role as perceived by the community at large ranges from *pendejo, tapao*, or *arrastrao* (*cachigranizo-roquenrolero* as they say in Mexico) to that of intellectual. The role has probably been all of these. From the perspective of the Chicano academic the role would probably be the same, for surely we have called ourselves these names.

Without being self-serving, I believe that the Chicano academic has fulfilled a fine role and has contributed to the academy as well as to the community. The question must be posed again. What has been the role and contribution to date? I believe the Chicano academic has made at least two significant contributions. One, the Chicano has opened and sensitized the academy to a degree. This is no small achievement and very difficult to do to an institution that is almost a thousand years old and which has survived pressures from every constituency possible. Two, the Chicano academic has aided in providing accessibility, as never before, into the academy for the community. The Chicano community will never be the same again because of this. A professional and middle class has been developing quickly: It is a middle class that may not have immediate ties to the older Chicano community but one that has affinities and loyalties far beyond those expressed before. To a large degree this was accomplished by the role that the Chicano academic has played in raising the level of consciousness in Chicano students.

The Chicano academic has aided significantly in making the Chicano community a legitimate entity. By having a presence in the academy, the Chicano academic ensured the presence of a Chicano community in curriculum development, in more sensitive student services, in better accessibility for Chicano students and faculty, in basic and applied research, and in the establishment of centers of study that focus on the kindred group. The Chicano academic aided the Chicano community in establishing itself, which is what the community wanted. This was not and is not a leisurely task; and it will become more complex and difficult.

Another question. What are the expectations of the Chicano community for Chicano academics? If we agree that the Chicano academic serves as a role model for the purpose of legitimizing the community, then the community has expected much. These expectations can be outlined under one word—leadership—all types of leadership: intellectual, social, political, cultural and economic. The Chicano community still has great faith in primary institutions and it still has much faith and pride in social secondary institutions as exemplified by higher education. It gains greatly psychologically when it sees its own human resourse as part of the academy. This brings a sense of well-being. This also places a great amount of pressure on the Chicano academic. The Chicano academic and the community understand that the only hope for the betterment of the community is better education. The Chicano academic wants to succeed, but he or she wants the community to succeed too. Likewise, the Chicano community wants the Chicano academic to succeed. Both want progress and betterment. Both want victories. It is important, then, for Chicano academics and communities to begin to establish real goals, to clarify priorities, to sacrifice even more energies, to have confidence and faith in the new generation of students and faculty and in the academy and ultimately in the total society.

What should be the role and contributions of the Chicano academic? He or she should first of all recognize the primary role of the academy. As a priority, it is most important to establish individual goals for *excellence* in teaching, research or creative activity and service to the academy. This is where the Chicano academic has the greatest possibility of success. This is what he or she has been educated and trained for. It is necessary that the Chicano academic establish a presence in the academy through excellence in these areas to offer an even better vision and service to the community. It is important that the Chicano academic work with the community from a position of strength. It is necessary that the Chicano academic work together with the community to define issues, plan strategies, and, most importantly, prioritize and assign responsibilities for community development. Within this context, Chicano academics should define individual goals with respect to leadership roles within the academy and outside it and when possible, leadership roles within the community. He or she should be conscious that the roles—be they intellectual, political, cultural, educational or social—may change quickly and may have lesser or major importance at any given moment. Thus the Chicano academic must always be willing to exchange current roles for others for which he or she is better suited and in which there is a greater opportunity to be effective regardless of peer pressures. In this respect the Chicano academic should be fiercely individualistic and independent.

The Chicano academic, in order to fulfill a dual role as academician and community leader, if he or she chooses, must maintain faith and will do so based on historical precedence and tradition. Angel Del Río, in his classic study of Spanish literature, states so well the preponderance of the Hispanic culture to dwell throughout centuries on the concept of a social democracy. The Chicano academic should keep in mind that his or her kindred group is not a newcomer to the process of higher education. Recent generations within the body politic of the U.S. are now being educated in greater numbers but Chicano intellectual traditions reach back to Salamanca, to Lima, to Mexico City through the Spanish language and to such scholars and creative people as Nezahualcóyotl, Maimónides, Averroes, Seneca and Vives. Chicano academics have an intellectual precedence on the American continent, to say nothing about the great and outstanding creative legacy of hundreds of years in Europe. The Chicano academic is a culmination of the Indo-Hispanic world that has evolved in the American republics as one of the world's greatest humanistic experiences—*mestizaje*. The Chicano academic is also part and parcel of the great intellectual traditions of other European countries and their outstanding universities. Most important, the Chicano academic is part of the great American university and the concept of mass education (perhaps the noblest experiment that any society has undertaken). American higher education is unequaled in the history of the world. It is an outstanding fact to note that the U.S. has over 3000 institutions of higher education. American higher education evolved a unique concept for the rest of the world by creating the land grant university, wherein a specific mission became service to the community. So the Chicano academic is well-positioned, well-trained and educated to contribute to the academy as well as to the community.

The community is not developing as well as other elements within American society. It demands leadership in all areas. It has problems and situations that need short and long range attention and solutions. The litany seems insurmountable. It is well known by Chicanos and non-Chicanos. Only the Native American ranks lower than the Chicano in educational achievement at the elementary, secondary and higher education levels, and in the ability to aggregate material wealth as well as physical and mental well-being. A nascent political power within the Chicano community brings much hope, but it is still weakened by a not well-educated mass. There are problems, such as immigration, that split the community. The community suffers from physical and mental stress. It increases demographically but the linkages and nets of influence which can aid in its development are far behind. In essence, the community gets more amorphous. Problems in unemployment, housing, civil rights, violence, mental health and so on are hindering a quicker development. But there has been a little progress, and there needs to be more.

The rest of this paper is divided into four sections:

1. Common Elements of Coherence Within Chicano Academics and the Chicano Community,
2. The Chicano Academic and the Academy: Contrasts and Struggles, Reasons and Faith,
3. The Changing Chicano Community: Its Perspective,
4. Directions, Goals, Strategies for Chicano Academics and Their Role Within the Chicano Community.

Common Elements of Coherence Within Chicano Academics and the Chicano Community

As a minority and heterogeneous group, it is important for the Chicano to constantly seek elements of coherence within the context of the broader society as well as within the Chicano community. By national public policy and by self-directed efforts the Chicano identifies with and is identified as coming from a specific community. Therefore the affinities to that community are constant. The Chicano academic shares many elements with the community. It is the place, the language and the values which have formed the first world view for the Chicano scholar. Even though he or she is part of academe, the following are part of his or her development and are common denominators among Chicano academics: the same community, for the most part the same working class parental background, and the same mixture of language (Spanish, English, Caló). The community from which the Chicano academic comes has been formed or distorted by the same political and economic forces. The same social forces have shaped the will or lack of will. The Chicano academic shares a common historical precedence and a clear presence. The Chicano academic shares a similar familial organizational structure, in essence the same personal voice of personal relationships. On the negative side, the larger society usually attributes a failure syndrome to the community as well as to the Chicano academic. This is far more negative than that which the Chicano academic attributes. In general, it is the culture of the community which prevails in the Chicano academic. In contrast with Anglo colleagues, one need only go over the preceding list to ask or indicate that the Anglo counterpart is not as preoccupied with the community as the Chicano. This is so in part because his or her community is constant as a right, as an accepted element, as a given. The Chicano community, on the other hand, is seen as questionable, as an error, as secondary in importance.

Chicano academics as well as the community have gone and are still going through a decolonization period. Many Chicano academics will recall the early 1960s when Chicano students and faculty would turn their heads away, full of embarrassment when someone would speak in Spanish and there were Anglos around. Also, there were notions that Anglo professors were more worthy of respect than Chicano professors, that Chicanos should not organize, for that would mean self-segregation—the worst of all evils in a democratic society. Expressions such as the following still ring in my head:

"We have to respect them."

"Why must we segregate ourselves, why must we organize?"

"There will be no school for the Mexicans beyond the eighth grade; they just don't have any aspirations for going to college."

"What are you doing getting a degree in English? Why don't you study to teach Spanish?"

"Say it in English."

"You got it made studying in Spanish. It's kind of immoral isn't it, to study what you already know?"

The Chicano academic must hold on to all the common denominators with the original community, for it's there that the sense of being and will are located. The community for the Chicano is the constant right, the accepted element and the given. Chicano academics without a tie to the Chicano community have very little. The intellectual precedence and transfer of culture demand a place of origin. This is where Richard Rodríguez is wrong and why he feels lonely and isolated.

The Chicano Academic and the Academy: Contrasts and Struggles, Reason and Faith

The Chicano in academia is a dichotomy, a quivering contrast with a judge-penitent attitude, who seeks answers for humanity, hoping somehow that what he or she effects does reach the community from whence he or she came. The Chicano lives in contrasts (*como una salamandra*) between the world of ideas, creativity, knowledge forefronts, and the realities of political and economic anemia of his or her community and a strong desire to change it. But Chicanos are just a bit more contrastive than their colleagues. Academics are contrastive people, period. They tend to be a tense group, at times timidly, apparently awaiting absolution, in an environment of reasoned struggles and filled with reason and faith. Within the institution, academics seek ideal perfections and gain comfort in structuring, knowing full well that termites can outdo them (with elegance) with their fecal droppings. The academic knows full well that outside the walls there exist imperfections and glaring errors. Inside, everything is rationalized—from racism to nuclear weapons, from Coors boycotts to disallowance of student evaluations, and even parking permits or tickets. Still, society provides. The Chicano academic partakes and becomes involved in the process, as he or she should. He or she is educated to survive the struggle. Society expects it.

> Today in our society certain fundamental struggles are under way. In academia this is reflected as a consequence. An example is the tension between technology and science on the one hand and the humanities and the arts on the other. Some twenty years ago, C. P. Snow gave his famous lecture on "The two cultures and the scientific revolution" wherein he recognized that the two cultures of the sciences and the humanities were separated seemingly by an intellectual and spiritual ocean.
>
> We have in our country a potentially disastrous condition. If our society were to become a society dominated by science and technology to the exclusion of the sense of history, social sensitivity, a spiritual aspect, or the creative arts, this certainly would be the case. This decade may see the emergence of machine intelligence. Science and technology have the capability to blur traditional distinctions between machines and human beings. The humanities and arts struggle to keep the human side dominant. They do so by pointing out the limitations of method, the exceptions to the law and the importance of intuition.
>
> What is unique about the university's relationship with the humanities and art and with science and technology is that the university's people insist on mixing things up, getting into the history of art, the social significance of the theatre, and so on. The university not only

forces the humanities and the arts, science and technology into contact with each other, but into contact with other fields of study—the aesthetics of engineering, the morality of law, the social psychology of medicine. The university is the place where studies count the most when they are done in relation to each other, where skills are acquired and utilized not as techniques but with concern for their meaning, effects and consequences.

Developing this special relationship between the university and the humanities and the arts or with science and technology, or bringing diverse specializations together, is never done easily and always done imperfectly. It is a struggle, and the fact that it is a struggle, involving the most serious elements of the university, working through the most consequential problems, is perhaps the best reason of a university (Martin, 1982).

The Chicano community has in the Chicano academic a well-trained element in this respect.

In learning theory there is what is called the perturbational theory of learning, meaning that creativity is encouraged and growth comes best out of tension and differences. Clearly the Chicano academic is part of this growth. As an educator he or she has structured struggles, has factored it to a personal equation, has relied on adversity and diversity of opinion and differences of perspectives to benefit everybody. Such is the cornerstone of the case for diversity in education. The well-being and advancement of society, educated people believe, requires a place where basic assumptions are examined, where alternatives are created, where minds weight options; a place where schools of thought are developed, where social, political and moral ramifications of thought are tested (Martin, 1982).

This is the work of the university. This is the work of the Chicano academic.

Society for its own sake, designates the university as a place where monumental struggles are not only tolerated but encouraged. Society delegates to trained minds the responsibility to think the unthinkable, regularly, so that on those occasions when society must assess its position and change direction, it will have resources for the task (Martin, 1982).

The Chicano academic should be considered by the community as that type of priceless resource. The Chicano academic is a trained mind. That in itself is an original element of positive power and strength.

The Changing Chicano Community: Its Perspective

From every perspective the Chicano community is changing. Studies indicate that it is basically an urban society, young and aggressive. Demographics indicate an accelerating population. The predictions of the early 1970s that there would be, by 1990, a total of seven cities on the U.S.-Mexican border with a population of more than a million have almost been realized. Clearly, by the year 2000 (that's only a generation away) there will be a total of fourteen cities within the border of the U.S. with a population of more than a million Chicanos/Hispanics. Ten of these will be in the American Southwest.

The Chicano community is a pluralistic society. It is a society in development, at different stages of educational, cultural, political and economic evolution. Yet there still persist some myths. The commercial and marketing opportunities that the community represents for business are fantastic. The business community now recognizes that the following are myths (Juárez, 1982):

Hispanics are monolingual;
Hispanics use only Spanish;
Hispanics are an unsegmented market;
Hispanic men make all major household decisions;

Hispanic women do not work;
the Hispanic market is only a temporary phenomenon due to unusually high legal and illegal immigration;
Hispanics will be absorbed into the American "mainstream" through language and cultural assimilation.

The corporate world has become increasingly interested in the Hispanic/Chicano population for future marketing reasons, and for control of these markets as part of their respective social action programs. In California, TRW, ARCO and FIBC have recently commissioned and completed reports dealing with the Hispanic/Chicano community.

The TRW/FIBC report done through SRI established the following:

1. Just about one in every five Californians is already Hispanic; and Hispanics will be the majority within a few decades.
2. Hispanics seek economic parity with Anglos on a community-wide, not just an individual, basis.
3. Hispanic and non-Hispanic leadership groups are frustrated with and angry at the failure of California's public school system to educate California's youth—Hispanic and non-Hispanic.
4. Hispanics and non-Hispanics agree English is essential for participation in California's future on an equal basis.
5. Hispanics believe large portions of the media—including papers like the Los Angeles Times and well-known movie personalities like Cheech and Chong—are biased and selective in their reporting on and portrayals of California Hispanics.
6. Hispanics do not believe that either the Democratic or the Republican party is interested enough in Hispanic objectives to accommodate Hispanic leaders within upper party echelons, to respond to Hispanic issues with a substantive party platform statement, or to organize Hispanic voters on a scale that would make them powerful.
7. Hispanics feel selectively cited for housing over-crowding vis-à-vis other immigrant groups, particularly Southeast Asians.
8. Hispanics see proposed cuts in human services as hurting them, but, in addition, as ending programs that have acted as a buffer between Hispanics and the government, thus making vigorous political action much more likely.
9. Hispanics and non-Hispanics feel local government, including the State government, must stop enforcing the rules of the U.S. Immigration and Naturalization Service.
10. Hispanics reject the idea that they must become exactly like Anglos in order to participate fully in California's economic, educational or political life.
11. Both Hispanic and non-Hispanic leaders want to find solutions to problems, not encourage increased fragmentation. These are avenues that can be taken now and further avenues that can be vigorously explored. The time to commence action is now.

ARCO sponsored an Aspen Institute in July 1981 in Baca, Colorado, titled *Hispanics and the Media*. The basic recommendations and action agenda from that meeting stipulated the following:

1. Increase and upgrade the employment of Latinos in the mass media, especially in editorial production, creative and performing roles;
2. Foster a balanced depiction of Latinos in the news and a full human range of Latino portrayal in entertainment fare;
3. Encourage *all* media professionals to be sensitive to the many parts played by Latinos in American life; and
4. Set hiring and promotion goals: A manager's performance in meeting these goals must be made a factor in periodic review of his or her own salary and advancement.

The Southern California Research Council (Occidental and Pomona Colleges), aided by some ten financial and industrial institutions in California, completed a study titled "Mexico and Southern California." Following are the general conclusions of that study (Southern California Research Council, 1981):

United States and Mexico Moving Toward a New Partnership

Past relations between the United States and Mexico have been characterized by misunderstanding, conflict, and even open hostility.

This legacy of suspicion is changing. Relations between the two countries may actually be taking a profound turn for the better.

Partnership Requires Mutual Understanding

Mexico's destiny has always been closely linked to the United States, even though the United States' focus has been directed primarily toward the Soviet Union, Europe and Japan.

Today, however, the United States finds its own future inextricably tied to Mexico's. Trade, energy and immigration are but a few vital issues linking our two countries.

We will not find solutions to our mutual problems unless we do more than merely deal with current issues. United States-Mexico relations are a product of the past, and what we can do about them is limited by perceptions stemming from our previous history.

Both the United States and Mexico expect, and deserve, to be treated with dignity, understanding and consideration by the other.

A Special Role for Business

Efforts to strengthen diplomatic ties between our two countries are important, but strengthening economic ties need not wait for political accord.

Indeed, it is economics and trade, more than politics and diplomacy that are improving United States-Mexico relations. The two countries need one another.

The leading edge in United States-Mexico relations is business in the United States working with business and government in Mexico. Total trade between the two countries increased by more than 48 percent in 1980. U.S. private investment in Mexico is growing rapidly, and technology transfer agreements, maquiladora assembly plants, border transactions, and tourism are increasing rapidly in importance.

A Special Relationship: Southern California and Mexico

Southern California is 50 percent more heavily involved than the rest of the United States in trade with Mexico. Southern California is similarly represented in other aspects of business and finance.

Our common heritage, our long-standing trading relationships, our complementary strengths and needs, and our proximity create for Southern California and Mexico a special relationship.

The Human Dimension: Undocumented Immigration

Immigration is a natural phenomenon when wage rates in one place greatly exceed those in another. Mexican immigration, in addition, is encouraged by geographic proximity, good transportation networks and social links between villages in Mexico and neighborhoods in the United States.

The impact of undocumented workers on unemployment, wages, and social services in the United States appears to be minimal.

Immigration of Mexican workers to the United States, despite certain serious problems, appears to be in the interest of both countries and the workers themselves.

The present system of undocumented immigration, for all its shortcomings, works reasonably well. It is difficult to find any improvements that will be politically acceptable either in the United States or Mexico. The present system of undocumented immigration appears to be preferable to a complicated, bureaucratic guest-worker program.

A Shared Future

The United States and Mexico face one another across the barrier of an international frontier, yet our cultures and economics are inescapably bound together and indeed flow into each other over that border. Nowhere is this more true than in the Southern California-Mexico border region.

Both the United States and Mexico face serious problems, the solutions for which require cooperation. Pursuing our mutual self-interest demands that we understand our evolving relationship. We must also approach one another with respect, patience and in a spirit of partnership.

The preceding reports have one thing in common. They were prepared with specific goals to understand and gauge the Mexican and Chicano potential as a market and as a common partner in business. The meetings that produced the reports were attended by Mexican and Chicano representatives. Therefore, the perceptions which were established were for the most part perceptions of Mexicans and Chicanos of their own communities.

One other report recently published is the report of the American Assembly on Mexican-American Relations. Among the many items discussed were trade and investment policies, energy, immigration, education, Mexico's role in the north-south dialogue and Central America, and specifically the Chicano community. The report states:

The participants feel that United States-Mexican relations will be increasingly affected by the growing proportion of persons of Mexican descent in the United States population, particularly in the Southwest and border regions, and by public attitudes toward this segment of the population. Because of this, it is particularly important that people of Mexican descent in the United States have equal social and economic opportunities while being permitted to retain their rich cultural heritage. In this regard, bilingual education and other bicultural programs to enhance and increase social and economic opportunities and to promote a mutual understanding and appreciation of both cultures should be encouraged. Similarly, the majority of participants agreed that not only is it not mutually exclusive for Mexican origin persons in the United States personally also to learn English and participate in the American mainstream, but indeed, all peoples in the United States and Mexico would benefit from such progress.

Given the tremendous growth already apparent and projected for the Southwest United States and Mexico, it is timely that we continue to develop a bicultural perspective which will make life better and more productive for all on both sides of the border (Regional American Assembly on Mexican-American Relations, 1981:10).

Directions, Goals, Strategies for Chicano Academics and Their Role Within the Chicano Community

The Chicano academic must do what he or she knows best. The first priority is to establish himself or herself as an authentic member of the academy. It is much easier and better to deal within the academy and in the community from a position of strength and authenticity. Professional development should be the number one priority. The Chicano community with its litany of issues and problems offers the Chicano academic every possible leadership opportunity. It is well that the Chicano academic gauge carefully what his or her role can be. The Chicano community is vibrant, changing and demanding. The Chicano academic is a rich resource for the community, for the academy itself is a place of struggle and tension which prepares the Chicano well for articulating change.

The following are some general goals and principles for the Chicano academic and the community. They are divided into two categories, educational and political, but probably these two categories should be one and the same.

Individually or collectively, the Chicano academic should press strongly for the following within the academy, within his or her institution or system:

1. Establish dialogue between institutions of higher education in order to clarify missions, share responsibilities, break down barriers, remove perceptual problems and begin to develop an integrated process of education from K-University.
2. Establish collaborative efforts between colleges or universities which have a high density of minority students and those that have a low density.
3. Establish cooperative efforts between research institutions and teaching institutions in order to ensure that the most talented minority faculty and students are reached.
4. Establish well-integrated cooperative efforts between community colleges, colleges, universities (public and private) that deal with remediation, basic skills, etc.
5. Accelerate the development of higher education councils (private and public) for the purpose of sharing resources, reviewing and studying economic development issues, and community development services.
6. Establish the accessibility of Chicanos into the academy (faculty and students) as the fundamental issue for the health of the total society which the institution serves.
7. Establish development programs for faculty, staff and management, that will raise the level of consciousness toward community development and student development.
8. Develop research that will define areas of commonalities among student populations.
9. Develop initiatives between the business community (Chicano and non-Chicano) and the university which will aid in the development of the Chicano community.
10. Ultimately, the responsibility for meeting the needs of students, faculty development, and indirectly, community development, is the responsibility of the chief executive officers of institutions of higher education. Sensitize and enlighten them. Help clarify for them the great need for development of the Chicano community. This community is of vast importance to the total society.

As for the political arena, it is important that the Chicano academic become involved in the political arena—at all levels—municipal, county, state and federal. The Chicano community does not yet have a strong public voice. Therefore it needs every voice it can garner. The voice should be intelligent, discriminating, judgemental. I believe Chicano academics have the potential to express such a voice. The Chicano academic should 1) seek to influence all levels of education, 2) encourage voter registration and participate vigorously in this endeavor, 3) enter into a non-personalismo leadership development, and 4) seek to define objectives for the Chicano community in conjunction with the emerging Chicano professional classes and with different elements of the Chicano community.

A strong political development for the Chicano community is necessary, but equally important, it should be a principled development. I believe this type of political development can be attained. The following are some principles that can affect and ensure this.

Some of these principles come from a speech by John Gardner, which he titled *The War of the Parts Against the Whole.*

1. The traditional and central functioning of government institutions is to reconcile multiple conflicting interests that cannot be reconciled elsewhere. The Chicano community must learn that it has that right.
2. As an organized group, the Chicano community should become more involved and

more concerned. It should also be concerned with the health of the political process. In part, all too often, it has been satisfied with disorganized, incompetent and even corrupt government thinking. The Chicano community and the Chicano academic must remember that a weak and corrupt government will sell out to rival interest groups just as cheerfully.

3. The Chicano academic should encourage the community to assist the effective and equitable functioning of government. Our political processes are designed to preside over peaceful competition of conflicting interests and to reconcile those interests within the framework of our shared purposes with the nation.

4. The Chicano academic role and the perceptions and the desires for the Chicano community should not be simply centrifugal forces of interest. The Chicano community must not neglect Commonweal priorities—because it is part of the Commonweal.

5. Neither the Chicano academic nor the Chicano community should regard compromise as betrayal although both must struggle fiercely.

6. The Chicano community is also the public, and it, as any other community, makes things workable or unworkable.

7. It is the responsibility of the Chicano academic and the Chicano community to develop and enhance their own potentialities. But this treasured autonomy and self-preoccupation also means that both should concern themselves with the common good. This is not idealism but mere self-preservation. The argument is not moralistic. If the large system fails, the subsystem fails. That is the reality. It should be understood that a society in which pluralism is not undergirded by some shared values and held together with some measure of mutual trust simply cannot survive. Pluralism that reflects no commitment to the common good is pluralism that ends in total divisiveness.

8. As a self-interest group, the Chicano community is part of the national life. It must keep its bargain with the society that gives it, as well as everyone else in our society, the freedom of the common good. It is important for the Chicano academic and for the Chicano community to reach out to other elements in American life to understand and to connect. There is power out there.

Closing: Reiterations

The priority for the Chicano academic should be to become a respected member of the academy through excellence in teaching, research or creative activity, and service. He or she will be able to deal better with all communities from a position of strength and will be more effective. The Chicano community needs leadership in many significant areas. Chicano academics can play any role they choose. It is important that the role be chosen carefully for effectiveness.

The Chicano community is changing drastically, expanding rapidly in numbers and becoming more amorphous. It is also becoming more vigorous. The Chicano academic should become part of the movement within the academy that is attempting to integrate philosophies and structures that will bring forth cooperative and collaborative efforts between all segments and levels of education from kindergarten through university education. This movement will surely affect the Chicano community.

The Chicano academic should get involved politically with the community. But the involvement should be principled. In the last analysis, the Chicano academic and the community will have to develop, as a priority, a *civic morality*. A civic morality gives clarity of action plus power and strength that become constant. It is only through this type of correct action that one can hope to build a better community. *Ni más, ni menos.*

My last thought pertains to the Chicano student in higher education. He or she is the link to the community. It is in the student that the Chicano academic should implant all good and correct ideas. The Chicano academic knows what these are. It is from the student that the Chicano academic regains those constant original elements from the community. The Chicano student's eyes still flicker with the passions of prophecy.

References

Gardner, J. W. "The War of the Parts Against the Whole." Presented on the occasion of his receiving the 17th Cosmos Club Award, Washington, D.C.

Juárez, N. "Marketing to Hispanics: Are You Relying on a Myth?" *Los Angeles Business Journal*, January 1982, 2-4.

Martin, W. B. "What Universities Do that Nobody Else Can." *Reports*, Association of Governing Board of Universities and Colleges, January-February 1982. 57-63.

Regional American Assembly on Mexican-American Relations. *Final Report of the Regional American Assembly on Mexican-American Relations*. November 1981. 10.

SRI International. *California Hispanics: A Report from the New Horizon Symposia*. Executive Summary. Menlo Park, California. ii, iii.

Southern California Research Council. Project Number 26: *Mexico and Southern California . . . Toward a New Partnership*. Claremont, California: Pomona College, 1981. 49-50.

INAUGURATION SPEECH
(April 28, 1980)

Chairman Reynolds, President Saxon, Mr. Boyer, distinguished platform guests and colleagues, representatives of sister institutions, UCR faculty, students, and staff, ladies and gentlemen.

I feel very fortunate today. My family is here. Many friends of our family are here, and I consider today's symbolic occasion a highlight in my life. I have many thanks to express to many people. Some are here today and some are not. I want to express thanks, too, to the many friends of our University and our campus. I am happy to see so many of them here today.

Relatively speaking, I have had a short career in administration, but already it has been complete with fine and excellent memories and sad and trying ones. It is already complete and full with ideas and people who have cared to be involved with what is still considered the most noble of efforts—the transmitting and discovery of knowledge, the urging and urge of acts of creativity, and the development of human resources.

Chairman Reynolds, and President Saxon, I am indeed proud to be part of the University of California. I am very, very proud to join the destiny of UCR.

There are many men and women of vision on this campus. Mr. Chairman, and Mr. President, I want to reiterate what you already know: On our campus we have some of the finest minds on earth. We also have some of the finest students on earth. This campus has dignity and pride. This comes from a history of critical and analytical effort on the part of its faculty to maintain excellence above everything else.

My nine months here have given me some of the finest moments of my life. I have had exalted ones when I have sensed the type of education that our students receive. I can see that they will make a difference in our society. Likewise, I feel exalted as I have come to learn of the very excellent research, both basic and applied, that our faculty carries out. I have noted the total efforts of our fine support staff and their pride in this campus.

My nine months here have given me some of the most trying moments also. We have people on our campus with courage and independence. To work with people of such independence is a most trying thing. I am personally glad to have this opportunity. (I am sure that my predecessors, Dr. Spieth and Dr. Hinderaker, would agree with me in this respect.) There is much to do here. There is much to develop. There will be some euphoria and much strain. We must get on with the job of the further development of UCR—its mission and its constituency.

To the faculty, students, and staff (to our campus constituency) I pledge to you the best of my efforts and energy. I also pledge to you that I will act fairly and with justice. I am committed to the further development of UCR as an institution with a full identity and as an institution that is second to none in its excellence.

Thank you.

COMMENCEMENT SPEECH, 1980:
REMEMBRANCE AND WILL

Vice President Blakely, Chancellor Hinderaker, platform guests, friends, colleagues, parents, and students, graduates to be. It is indeed a great pleasure to be here and participate with you in your commencement. I want to thank, especially, Chancellor Hinderaker for the invitation to be here with you today and thank him for giving my wife and me, in such few days, their enthusiasm, their vision and their wisdom of their last 15 years.

In our ordeals of civility a commencement is without question one of the richest and most moving rituals. To see a sea of uniform smiles and academic regalia always calls for applause and congratulations.

I chose the title "Remembrance and Will" because a commencement is not only an official act of termination and beginning but also a recollection, a remembrance, and the will. I recall that I was once asked to list a group of words that contain the most general human positive qualities or perceptions—love, beauty, integrity, excellence, etc., courage, honesty, wisdom, etc. These are human qualities for which we strive, which we respect, which hold civilizations together. What nurtures all civil endeavors positively is the will, the volition for these very qualities to continue.

Emerson states in one of his many brilliant essays on states that all men live lives of quiet desperation. Life is remembering. Life is the will to continue. In the years ahead you will be in desperate moments, you will enjoy beautiful moments, and you will be inert. You will be disenchanted with the human species. I am sure you have had these types of moments already, but you will have more.

Anytime that your being is unbalanced by negativeness by the erosion of your will I ask that you recur to your ability to remember to recollect your life, yourself. From that remembrance will come forth the will to continue, to survive, to restructure, the will to be again and again. I do not mean to imply in any way to be self-indulgent. I do mean to seek in your memory, to search in your memory for those acts of volition which clearly invented you with others in awe of the common elements, the original elements which we all possess such as those I have mentioned in the previous sentence.

These common elements are values structured by that ordeal called civility—one of the many definitions of the word culture. Every person has the basic potential to recollect himself/herself. Indeed in all civilizations (whether we label them primitive or advanced) the most evident drive is the urge of the members of these civilizatoins to recollect, to document or to remember their efforts to give form to individual and collective memory. Recollection keeps the folk cultures alive. So-called primitive civilizations survive because of re-collective efforts. Society has cared to recollect and to pass on the individual and collective spirit by narrative—be it song, anecdote, singular symbol, etc. We as individuals are the very *recapitación* of century upon century of molding. It is, this recollection, a sacred gift.

What to remember?

1. Your personal search and discovery and points of eureka in your life. How intense has your urge been? How labyrinthian? Do you still have the passion of self-prophecy? Recollect and reflect on these.

2. Your human passions. Recollect the crystallization of these passions—hate, envy, love, kindness, fears, knowlege. Sense these and gain wisdom from this urge to crystallize.

3. Your gift to others. Surely you have been generous with helping, aiding others, young, old, your age. Recollect those instances in which you were thoughtful, considerate and when you gave of your perceptions, of your energies for the common good. Indeed the one outstanding collective characteristic of our nation is our civic morality. What has been your effort in this regard toward community, region, nation and mankind?

4. Your friends and family. If life is an invention, with whom have you invented yourself? Recollect those moments when you clearly sensed that life was a relationship. Certainly the first important relationship is your very own family. Parents who have given you the very positive and elementary values of your civilization. It is your turn to provide these to friends and family. Your friends, remember your friends, they have provided a reflection too, they have given you an identity.

5. As individuals we are finite. We are, when reduced to this finite, a thought process, a relationship. We are also an anecdote, an invention, a *recaptación de vida,* a discovery. Finally we are a memory.

6. A commencement besides a beginning and an official act is a ritual for the recollection of many thoughts. Today as you await a final act, spend a few moments of reflection upon the many events, stresses, that led you here. Do this time and again. I am sure you will gain some sustenance of will. The will to act with judgment, to create, to sense the bind with mankind, and essentially to be.

Be sure that along the way you have become a memory and a sense of volition for so many.

Best wishes to each one of you.
Thank you.

Webster, Texas
Noviembre 17,1963

Dr. Luis Leal
Department of Spanish and Italian
University of Illinois
Urbana , Illinois

Estimado Profesor Leal ;

La presente va con un fuerte y sincero saludo. Espero que
al recibir esta esté disfrutando de todo en general. Durante
el tiempo que estudié bajo usted en Guadalajara este verano
pasado me fui interesando intensamente en la literatura hispanoamericana. Le escribo porque siento que puedo confiar en usted
y en su sinceridad.

Deseo estudiar la literatura hispanoamericana y la cultura hispanoamericana a fondo. Si es posible me gustaría estudiar bajo
usted . Cuando obtuve el grado de bachiller me incliné a la
literatura inglesa. Sin embargo he enseñado la lengua española
durante los últimos seis años. El próximo verano recibiré el
grado de grado de maestro en educación con menores en inglés y
español.

Si es posible quisiera que me indicara si su universidad tiene
algunas becas que yo podría obtener y si las hay , sus requisitos.
Mis mas hondos deseos siempre han sido de seguir estudiando hasta
el doctorado en la literatura hispanoamericana.

Su clase de literatura durante el verano pasado me agrado infinitamente.
Espero que algún día pueda tener la oportunidad de escucharle
sus conferencias sobre la literatura hispanoamericana.

Atentamente ,

Tomás Rivera
Tomás Rivera
306 Hubert Street
Webster, Texas

THE UNIVERSITY OF TEXAS AT SAN ANTONIO
SAN ANTONIO, TEXAS 78285

OFFICE OF THE PRESIDENT

June 9, 1976

Dr. Luis Leal
University of Illinois
College of Liberal Arts & Sciences
Dept. of Spanish, Italian and Portuguese
4080 Foreign Languages Bldg.
Urbana, Illinois 61801

Querido don Luis,

Gracias por la separata que me mandó. Lamento que no pueda estar
con nosotros en Floricanto III. Desde luego que estará su espíritu.
Como le he dicho anteriormente, en lo que va de mi parte, yo
aprendí de usted toda la técnica del cuento. Así que lo que me
enseñó aquel verano en Guadalajara ha sido de gran significado en mi
propia carrera no solo de cuentista sino de profesor. Lo que me
enseñó se lo sigo pasando a mis estudiantes. Gracias por sus
comentarios sobre "Salamandras."

Pues, hasta la próxima. Cuando esté o pase por San Antonio, por
favor comuníquese conmigo. Aquí tiene su casa y una amistad
sincera.

Un abrazo,

Tomás Rivera
Vice President for Administration

jah

THE UNIVERSITY OF TEXAS AT SAN ANTONIO
SAN ANTONIO, TEXAS 78285
512 — 691-4120

VICE PRESIDENT FOR ADMINISTRATION   23 de mayo 1978

Prof. Americo Paredes
Center for Mexican American Studies
Student Services Building 307
The University of Texas at Austin
Austin, Texas 78712

Estimado Américo,

Recibí la separata, "On Ethnographic Work Among Minority Groups,"
que me mandaste y quiero darte las más sinceras gracias por medio
de ésta. La he leído con gran interés como siempre lo hago con
cualquier trabajo tuyo.

Aún recuerdo el instante, hace ya unos veinte años, cuando leí
con su pistola... y como anduve por días con el regocijo secreto de
que por fin había descubierto algo que era propiamente nuestro.
Haz sido fuente intelectual y espiritual para muchos de nosotros.

Un abrazo,

Tomás Rivera

jah

The University of Texas at El Paso

Executive Vice President

October 10, 1978

Professor Rolando Hinojosa
Chicano Studies
University of Minnesota - Twin Cities
489 Ford Hall
224 Church Street S.E.
Minneapolis, Minn. 55455

Estimado Rolando:

He recibido todo lo que me has mandado pero como te contaré algún día he
estado muy ocupado con muchas cosas, algunas interesantes y algunas, las que
se llevan mas tiempo, de la chigada. Pero el mundo sigue su marcha con Haste.
He leido tanto que me has mandado y quiero felicitarte por tu gran empeño
y más que todo por tu talentazo. Aun me acuerdo cuando me ponías a dormir
allá por el '72 en San Francisco en el hotelazo aquel dondo nos dieron
descuento porque traía yo una tarjeta de agente viajero - y Rafa en el
elevador, perdón ascensor, guachando la nalga. Nalgame Dios, como se pasa
el tiempo.

Según llamadas y aceptaciones nos veremos en Davis, California en un mes.
Y tengo mucho que platicarte. Ya sabes, tan pronto que Guggenheim me pida
carta, luego, luego. Animo. La nota sobre la publicación de Klail en
Alemania me dio mucho gusto, Rolando. Y por muchas razones, por tí, tu
familia, por la raza, por mí, etc.

Bueno, pues, a ver si más alla tengo chanza de mandarte otras letras. Por
aquí pasó un ventarron que venía de Las cruces el jueves pasado, dejó el olor
de azufre.

un abrazo,

Tomás

STATEMENT OF PERSONAL OUTLOOK ON THE FUTURE
OF AMERICAN HIGHER EDUCATION

We are still in the threshold of accessibility to academe for all Americans, that is, Americans from all strata of society and academic preparation. Likewise we are in a period of an even more increased need for education. We seem to believe strongly in an American ideal that life is education. The demand for education, however, may cloud completely the reasons for it. Is education necessary only for the attainment of jobs and security? Is education for the purpose of attainment of the inherent wisdom of mankind? In the last analysis higher education is the last defense in maintaining our nation's great belief in civic morality. I believe this to be the greatest challenge to academe. We need to take care to ensure that our institutions of higher education provide our country with this impetus. I am optimistic that higher education will continue to give our citizens better societal and natural resource managers and more importantly, continue to impart to our citizens that education is also the gaining of wisdom. To maintain these attitudes is, in my perspective, much more important than any process, system, etc., that we may need to devise to carry out the objectives.

UNIVERSITY OF CALIFORNIA, RIVERSIDE

BERKELEY • DAVIS • IRVINE • LOS ANGELES • RIVERSIDE • SAN DIEGO • SAN FRANCISCO   SANTA BARBARA • SANTA CRUZ

OFFICE OF THE CHANCELLOR
RIVERSIDE, CALIFORNIA 92521

April, 1980

Estimados amigos:

My basic preoccupation and philosophy is that all our community receive the highest quality of education. We need this in order for our society to survive.

Within this context, it is imperative that the total hispanic community receive the highest quality of education. This type of education was necessary for our past generations and for the most part we did not get it. This type of education is even more important for the present generations of hispanic students who are now in school--kindergarten through graduate and professional.

We, as hispanics, have many traditions. The most progressive have always been our basic trust in primary institutions such as the family. Also, we have always had an almost blind trust in our secondary institutions, be they educational, political, etc., etc. I urge you to continue with that trust in secondary institutions, but with open eyes.

In order to have access to the best that our country has to provide, it is necessary not only to demand, but more importantly, to lead and to become passionately involved in the processes. Trusting, demanding, leading, and involvement are all natural corollaries for improvement, progress, and strength in community development.

A high quality education provided at all levels for the hispanic communities will ensure stronger individuals, and in turn, a stronger community. This type of education must be one of our constant and basic demands. We can only ensure this education if we lead, if we become involved in getting it, if we have trust in it, and most importantly, if we make it part of our prophesy.

My best wishes are with you.

Atentamente,

Tomás Rivera
Chancellor

III. The Professional Life of Tomás Rivera

Updated 03/27/84

CURRICULUM VITA
Tomás Rivera

Personal Data

Business Address: Office of the Chancellor
University of California, Riverside
Riverside, CA 92521
Phone: 714-787-5201

4171 Watkins Drive
Riverside, CA 92507
Phone: 714-683-7837

Birthplace: Crystal City, Texas
Birthdate: December 22, 1935
Family Status: Married; wife—Concepción; daughters—
    Ileana, 23; Irasema, 22;
    son—Javier, 16
Soc. Sec. No.   466-54-7029

Education

Ph.D   (Romance Languages and Literature), University of Oklahoma, 1969.

M.A.   (Spanish Literature; minors: French Literature, Spanish, and American Literature), University of Oklahoma, 1969.

M.Ed.   (Educational Administration; minors: English, Spanish), Southwest Texas State University, 1964.

B.S.   (Ed.), (Major: English; minors: Spanish, History, Education), Southwest Texas State University, 1958.

A.A.   (Major: English), Southwest Texas Jr. College, 1956.

Diploma   Crystal City High School, Crystal City, Texas. 1954.

Other Preparations

NDEA Spanish Institute Level I   University of Arizona, Guadalajara, Jalisco, Mexico, 1963

NDEA Spanish Institute Level I   University of Texas at Austin, 1962.

Employment Record

7/79-Present	Chancellor, University of California, Riverside; (and Professor of Romance Languages and Literatures).
2/80-Present	Corporate Officer, Times Mirror Company.
9/78-7/79	Executive Vice President and Acting Vice President for Academic Affairs, University of Texas at El Paso (and Professor of Spanish).
3/76-9/78	Vice President for Administration, University of Texas at San Antonio (and Professor of Spanish).
1/73-3/76	Associate Dean, College of Multidisciplinary Studies, and Professor of Spanish, University of Texas at San Antonio.
9/71-1/73	Director, Division of Foreign Languages, Literature and Linguistics, College of Humanities and Social Sciences, and Professor of Spanish Literature, University of Texas at San Antonio.
1972-73	Visiting Professor of Spanish (part-time), Trinity University, San Antonio, Texas.
1969-71	Associate Professor of Spanish, Sam Houston State University.
Summers 1971 & 1970	Teacher, Mexican Field School, Puebla, Mexico, program of Sam Houston State University.
Summer 1969	Assistant Director, Spanish Studies Program in Madrid, University of Oklahoma.
1968-69	Instructor Director, Language Laboratories, University of Oklahoma.
1966-68	Teaching Assistant, Department of Modern Languages; and Lecturer on Migrant problems in VISTA training program, Multi-purpose Training Center, University of Oklahoma.
1965-66	Chairman and Instructor, Department of Foreign Languages, Southwest Texas Jr. College.
1960-65	Spanish Teacher, Secondary, Clear Creek I.S.D., League City, Texas.
1958-60	Spanish Teacher, Secondary, Crystal City I.S.D., Crystal City, Texas.
1957-58	English Teacher, Secondary, Edgewood I.S.D., San Antonio, Texas.
Prior	Up to the time I started my teaching career, I was part of the migrant labor stream that went from Texas to various parts of the Midwest. I lived and worked in Iowa, Minnesota, Wisconsin, Michigan, and North Dakota.

Professional service   I am or have been a member of the following:

Executive Committee, Western College Association, April 1983 to present.

Board of Trustees, Carnegie Foundation for the Advancement of Teaching, 1978-1982; elected to a second 4-year term, 1982-1986.

Board of Trustees, Educational Testing Services, elected for 1980-1984 period.

Board of Directors, American Association for Higher Education, 1981 to present.

Founding Member, Member of Executive Committee, National Council of Chicanos in Higher Education, 1976 to present; also Vice President 1978-present.

Board of Directors, American Council on Education, October 1980 to Oct. 1982.

Board of Foreign Scholarships, U.S. Department of State; International Communication Agency; (Presidential appointment) Fulbright Program, 1978-1981.

Advisory Board, American Council on Education's Educational Record, February 1980 to present.

Task Force in the Hispanic Arts, National Endowment for the Arts, 1977-1979.

Board of Advisors, Modern Language Association of America, July 1980 to present.

Council on Entrance Services, College Entrance Examination Board, 1976-1980.

Contributing Editor, MELUS, 1977-1979.

Inland Empire Higher Education Council, 1979 to present; President, 1981-1982.

Board of Trustees, Institute for the Humanities at Salado (Texas), June 1980 to present.

Scholar team for "Bless Me, Ultima" Project, Ruiz Productions, Inc., June 1980 to present.

Advisory Committee, Association of Southwestern Humanities Councils, January 1980 to present.

Judge, Shelley Memorial Award for Poetry, 1980, 1983.

Board, National Center for Higher Educational Management Systems, 1979.

Advisory Committee, *La Historia* (a projected series of eight one-hour dramas, to be produced by KCET, Channel 28, for national airing on PBS), 1979 to present.

Board, Texas Commission on the Humanities, 1979 (moved from Texas and could not serve).

Member, Selection Committee, Ford Foundation Graduate Fellowship for Mexican Americans, 1973-1975; Chairman, 1974-1975.

Judge, Chicano Writing Contest, University of California, Irvine, 1975, 1977, 1978 (fiction and poetry).

Judge, San Antonio Public Library Poetry Award, *Pegasus*, 1975, 1976, 1977, 1978.

Judge, Poetry Contest, *Caracol*, San Antonio, 1976.

Judge, Playwriting Contest, *Caracol*, San Antonio, 1975.

Chairman, Board of Directors, *Tejidos*, Austin, Texas, Spring, 1975.

Contributing Editor, *Revista Chicano-Riqueña*, Indiana University, 1972 to present. (The *Revista* is now housed at University of Houston.)

Contributing Editor, *El Grito*, Quinto Sol Publications, Berkeley, California, 1972-1975.

Board of Directors, MICTLA Publications, El Paso, Texas, 1972-1973.

Board of Directors, *El Magazín*, San Antonio, Texas, 1971-1973.

Board of Directors, Pan-American Student Forum, 1965.

Professional Memberships

American Association of University Professors

Associated Writing Programs

Modern Language Association

Latin American Studies Association

Public Service

Member, National Commission on College Retirement, The Carnegie Corporation, 1984 to present.

Member, Committee on Opportunities in Science, American Association for the Advancement of Science, November 1983 to present.

Member, National Commission on Secondary Schooling for Hispanics, October 1983 to present.

Member, Council on Foreign Relations, February 1983 to present.

Member, President's Commission on a National Agenda for the Eighties. July 1980 through December 1980 (Presidential appointment).

Member, Carnegie Commission on the Future of Public Broadcasting, 1977 to 1979.

Member, Board of Directors, National Hispanic Scholarship Fund, 1979 to present.

Member, Advisory Committee, Human Resources Management and Development Program, October 26, 1979 to present.

Member, Board, Hubert H. Humphrey Institute for Public Affairs, University of Minnesota, 1979.

Member, Advisory Board, Southwest Board Regional Commission, 1979 to 1981 (Governor's appointment, State of California).

Member, Advisory Board, American Tropical Mural Conservation Committee, April 1980 to present.

Member, Advisory Committee, Allied Health Professions' Coordinating Board, University and College System of Texas, 1979.

Member, Board of Trustees, Citizens' Goals for Greater Riverside Area, December 1981 to present.

Member, Board of Directors, Riverside Community Hospital Corporation, April 1981 to April 1982.

Member, Board of Greater Riverside Chambers of Commerce, 1981 to present.

Member, Greater Riverside Hispanic Chamber of Commerce, 1981 to present.

Member, Executive Board, Inland Empire Council, Boy Scouts of America, 1981.

Member, Board of Directors, American Issue Forum, City of San Antonio, Texas, 1975-1976.

Member, Bexar County Historical Society, 1975-1977 (by appointment).

Member, Board of Directors, San Antonio Easter Seal Society, 1977.

Member, Sustaining Fund Committee, Mexican-American Cultural Center, 1977-1979.

Member, Advisory Board, Religious Communities for the Arts, Annual Conference, San Antonio, Texas, May 1978.

Member, Board of Directors, Association for the Advancement of Mexican Americans, Houston, Texas, 1977-1979.

Honors, Awards, Recognitions

Académico Correspondiente, Academia Norteamericana de la Lengua Española, New York, New York, February 1984.

NAACP'er of the Year Award, Riverside, California, February 1984.

First Robert D. Clark Distinguished Visiting Professor, San Jose State University, San Jose, California, May 1983

H.L.D., (Honoris Causa-Doctorate of Humane Letters), Western New Mexico Univ., May 1982.

Ed.D., (Honoris Causa), University of Santa Clara, June 1980.

Honored by the California Chicano News Media Association for outstanding achievements and contributions to the Chicano community, July 1982.

Outstanding Chicano Educator, 1981, *Caminos Magazine*, Los Angeles.

Distinguished Alumnus Award, Southwest Texas State University, San Marcos, Texas, February 1981.

Pacesetter Award, Inland Area Urban League, Riverside-San Bernardino, California, January 31, 1981.

Invited Member, Hispanic Corporate Board Members, Personnel Management Association of Aztlán, June 18, 1980 to present.

Honorary Member, Phi Beta Kappa, Iota Chapter, Riverside, California, May 1980 to present. (In recognition of contributions to the field of literature).

Honorary Member, Phi Delta Kappa, Riverside Chapter, 1979 to present.

Honorary Member, Rotary Club, Riverside, California, December 1979.

Recipient, Annual Project Milestone Recognition Award, National Conference Association
  for Supervision and Curriculum Development, Houston, Texas, March 22, 1977.
Honorary Member, Kiwanis International, 1976.
Sembrador of the Year, Outstanding Citizen of San Antonio, 1974. (Club Sembradores de
  Amistad, for Outstanding and meritorious service to the community 1974-1975).
Danforth Foundation Associateship (husband and wife), 1971.
Recipient, *Premio Quinto Sol*, National Literary Award for best work, 1970-1971.
Member and President, Sigma Delta Pi, University of Oklahoma, 1968.
Member, Phi Theta Kappa, 1956.

Listed in:

Marquis' *Who's Who in America,* 41st edition, 1980; 42nd edition, 1983.
Directory of American Scholars, Vol. III, 1978.
Change Magazine ("100 Young Academic Leaders"), 1978.
Directory of American Fiction Writers, 1975.
Contemporary Authors, 1974.
International Who's Who in Poetry, Spring, 1974.
A Directory of American Poets, 1974.
Personalities of the South, 1973.
Directory of Mexican-Americanists, 1970.

Papers and Presentations

Over the years I have made numerous presentations as formal papers, as symposia and
workshop or consultantship contributions, as well as formal and informal speeches. About
one-half of the formal papers have been related to the education of the Mexican-American;
about one-half have concerned Spanish-American and Mexican-American literature. The
formal presentations have been at regional, state, national, and international professional
meetings and at literary symposia at different U.S. universities. Listed below are selected
professional meetings, universities, and consultantships where the presentations were given:

Professional Organizations (presentations of formal papers)

Council of Hispanic American Ministries (national).
Association for Supervision and Curriculum Development (national).
Texas State Teachers' Association (regional and state).
American Personnel and Guidance Association (national).
Texas Foreign Language Association (state).
American Association of Teachers of Spanish and Portuguese (national).
AATSP Alamo Valley (regional and state).
Southwestern Sociological Association (regional).
Texas Association of Financial Aid Officers (state).
College Composition and Communication Conference (national).
National Federation of Settlements and Neighborhood Centers (national).
National Council of Teachers of English (national).
Modern Language Association (national).
National Institute of Health (national).
Popular Culture Association (national).
XVI Congreso del Instituto Internacional de Literatura Iberoamericana (international).
Texas Association of Chicanos in Higher Education (state).
IMAGE State Convention (Texas).

Cal/Neva Community Actional Association, 1980 (regional).
American Association for Higher Education, 1982 (national).

Consultantships: Education, Culture, and Literature and Language Arts

Ford Foundation, 1973-1975 (Chairman, Selection Committee for Graduate Fellowships for Mexican-Americans)
Antioch College
Pharr-San Juan-Alamo Independent School District, Pharr, TX
Development Associates, Inc.
Northeast Independent School District, San Antonio, TX
Northside Independent School District, San Antonio, TX
Bryan Independent School District, Bryan, TX
Crystal City Independent School District, Crystal City, TX
West Texas Education Center, Region VI, Odessa, TX
Education Service Center, Region II, Kingsville, TX
South San Antonio Independent School District, San Antonio, TX
Education Service Center, Region XIII, Austin, TX
Education Service Center, Region I, McAllen, TX
Intercultural Development Research Associates, San Antonio, TX
Rio Hondo Independent School District, Rio Hondo, TX
Austin Independent School District, Austin, TX
Harlandale Independent School District, San Antonio, TX
Seguin Independent School District, Seguin, TX
Carrascolendas—Center for Communication Research, University of Texas at Austin
Southwest Mobile Institute
Center for Public School Ethnic Studies—University of Texas at Austin
PAUTA (Pan-American University and University of Texas at Austin Administrative Program)
U.S. Office of Education, OFE, 1970
Texas Education Agency (Accreditation Team, Dallas Baptist College and Prairie View A and M)
Mexican-American Cultural Center, San Antonio, TX
Centro Video, Oblate College, San Antonio, TX
Southwest Intergovernmental Training Center, San Antonio, TX
Riverside County Superintendent of Schools Multicultural Conference, Riverside, CA
League of United Latin American Citizens, Symposium, Washington, D.C.

Universities—Literary Symposia

I have presented professional papers at the following universities:

Austin College	Trinity University, Texas
Brigham Young University	Tulane University
California State University, Fullerton	Universidad de Las Américas, Cholula
California State University, Sacramento	University of Arizona
California State University, San Diego	University of California, Berkeley
Central Michigan University	University of California, Davis
Colorado College, Colorado Springs	University of California, Irvine
El Paso Community College, Colorado	University of California, Los Angeles
Incarnate Word College	University of California, San Diego
Indiana University, Bloomington	University of California, Santa Barbara
Merritt College	University of California, Santa Cruz

Michigan State University
New Mexico State University
Our Lady of the Lake University
Pan American University
Rice University
Sam Houston State University
San Antonio College
Southern Methodist University
Southwest Texas Junior College
Southwest Texas State University
Stanford University
Texas A and I University
Texas Lutheran College
Texas Technological University

University of Colorado, Boulder
University of Colorado, Denver
University of Houston
University of Indiana, Northwest
University of Michigan
University of Nebraska
University of Oklahoma
University of Pennsylvania
University of Southern California
University of Texas at Austin
University of Texas at El Paso
University of Utah
University of Wisconsin, Madison
Yale University
Universidad Nacional Autónoma de México

Publications

Books

La ideología del hombre en la obra poética de León Felipe. Ann Arbor, D.A., 1969, 156 pp.

"*. . . y no se lo tragó la tierra/And the Earth Did not Part.*" Quinto Sol Publications, Berkeley, 1971, xxii + 117 pp. [Novel.]

[Revised ed. Translation and Introduction by Herminio Ríos C., Editorial Justa, Berkeley, California, 1976.]

Always and Other Poems. Sisterdale Press, Sisterdale, Texas, 1973, 15 pp.

La casa grande del pueblo. (Forthcoming with Justa Publications.) 357 pp. [Novel.]

Excerpts

"El año perdido/The Lost Year" and ". . . y no se lo tragó la tierra/. . . and the earth did not part." *El Grito*, 4, 2 (Winter 1971), pp. 9-21.

"La mano en la bolsa/His Hand in His Pocket" and ". . . y no se lo tragó la tierra/. . . and the earth did not part." Trans. Herminio Ríos C. in *El espejo/The Mirror.* Eds. Octavio Ignacio Romano-V. and Herminio Ríos C.

[Revised ed. Quinto Sol, Berkeley, California, 1972, pp. 15-40.]

"Debajo de la casa." *El Magazín*, 1, 8 (February 1973), pp. 68-70.

"La cara en el espejo." In *Festival Flor y Canto II: An Anthology of Chicano Literature from the Festival* held March 12-16, 1975, Austin, Texas. Eds. Arnold C. Vento, Alurista, and José Flores Peregrino. Pajarito Publications, Albuquerque, New Mexico, 1979, pp. 122-24.

"Los niños no se aguantaron" and "Un rezo." In *El Quetzal Emplumece.* Eds. Carmela Montalvo, Leonardo Anguiano, and Cecilio García-Camarillo. Mexican American Cultural Center, San Antonio, Texas, 1976, pp. 434-35.

"Inside the Window." *Caracol*, 3, 12 (August 1977), pp. 17-18.

"The Portrait." In *Ideas*, Vol. 6, *Focus on Literature.* Eds. Philip McFarland et al., Houghton Mifflin, Boston, 1978, pp. 145-48.

[Also in *The United States in Literature.* Eds. Cárdenas et al., Scott-Foresman, 1978.]

Short Stories

"Eva y Daniel/Eva and Daniel" *El Grito*, 5, 3 (Spring 1972), pp. 18-25.

[Reprint (English only) in *English in Texas* (Texas Joint Council of Teachers of English), 10, 2 (Winter 1978), pp. 38-39.]

[Reprint in *Nuevos Horizontes*, Eds. José B. Fernández and Nasario García. D. C. Heath and Company, Lexington, Massachusetts, 1982.]

"On the Road to Texas: Pete Fonseca." *Aztlán: An Anthology of Mexican American Literature*. Eds. Luis Valdez and Stan Steiner, Alfred A. Knopf, New York, 1972, pp. 146-54.

[Reprint in *Voices of Aztlán: Chicano Literature of Today*. Eds. Dorothy E. Harth and Lewis M. Baldwin, New American Library, New York, 1974, pp. 52-58.]

[Reprint (in Spanish) as "El Pete Fonseca," *Revista Chicano-Riqueña*, 2, 1, (Winter 1974), 15-22.]

[Reprint (in Spanish) as "El Pete Fonseca," *A Decade of Hispanic Literature: An Anniversary Anthology*, Revista Chicano-Riqueña, Houston, 1982.]

"Looking for Borges," *Revista Chicano-Riqueña*, 1, 1 (Spring 1973), pp. 2-4.

[Reprint (in Spanish) as "En busca de Borges," *Caracol*, 1, 10 (June 1975), pp. 14-15.]

[Reprint in *Kaleidoscopia* (Univ. de las Américas), Summer 1975.]

"Las salamandras," *Mester*, 5, 1 (November 1974), pp. 25-26.

[Reprint as "Salamandra," *Caracol*, 1, 6 (February 1975), pp. 14-16.]

[Reprint in *Kaleidoscopia* (Univ. de las Américas), Summer 1975.]

[Reprint in *El Cuento: Revista de la Imaginación*, No. 70, (July-December 1975), pp. 379-81.]

[Reprint in *Festival de Flor y Canto I: An Anthology of Chicano Literature*. Eds. Alurista et al., University of Southern California, Los Angeles, California, 1976, pp. 22-23.]

Poetry

"Me lo enterraron," *Original Works, A Foreign Language Quarterly* (1967), p. 10.

"De niño, de joven, de viejo," "Hide the Old People, or American Idearium," "Me lo enterraron," "M'ijo no mira nada," "Odio," "The Rooster Crows en Iowa y en Texas," and "Siempre el domingo," *El Grito*, 3, 1 (Fall 1969), pp. 56-63.

[Reprint in *El Espejo/The Mirror*. Eds. Octavio Ignacio Romano-V. and Herminio Ríos C. Revised ed. Quinto Sol, Berkeley, California, 1972, pp. 237-44.]

"Young Voices," *Songs and Dreams*. Ed. Joseph A. Flores, Pendulum Press, West Haven, Connecticut, 1972, p. 80.

Always and Other Poems. Sisterdale Press, Sisterdale, Texas, 1973, 15 pp. (Also listed under books.)

"The Eyes of a Child," "Past Possessions," "Soundless Words," and "When Love to Be?" in *We are Chicanos: An Anthology of Mexican-American Literature*. Ed. Philip D. Ortego, Washington Square Press, New York, 1973, pp. 184-87.

"The Child," "When Love to Be?" and "Young Voices," *Revista Chicano-Riqueña*, 1, 1 (Spring 1973), pp. 17-18.

[Reprint with "The Rooster Crows en Iowa y en Texas," *English in Texas* (Texas Joint Council of Teachers of English), 10, 2 (Winter 1978), pp. 33, 35.]

"M'ijo no mira nada," "The Overalls," "The Rooster Crows en Iowa y en Texas," and "Siempre el domingo," *The New Breed: An Anthology of Texas Poets*. Ed. David Oliphant, Prickly Pear Press, Malta, Illinois, 1973, pp. 138-43.

"Alone," "Always," "The Overalls," and "Soundless Words," *Café Solo*. Ed. Glenna Luschei, Solo Press, San Luis Obispo, California, 1974, pp. 3132.

"The Searchers," *Ethnic Literatures since 1776: The Many Voices of America*. Eds. Wolodymyr T. Zyla and Wendell M. Aycock, *Proceedings of Comparative Literature Symposium*, Texas Tech. Press, Lubbock, Texas, 1976, pp. 27-31.

"De niño, de joven, de viejo," "Hide the Old People, or American Idearium," "Me lo enterraron," "M'ijo no mira nada," "A Most Tired Word," "Odio," "The Rooster Crows en Iowa y en Texas," "Run, Puff, Run, Run," "Siempre el domingo," "Soundless Words," and "This Solitude." *El Quetzal Emplumece*. Eds. Carmela Montalvo, Leonardo Anguiano, and Cecilio García-Camarillo, Mexican-American Cultural Center, San Antonio, Texas, 1976, pp. 246-53.

"A Blas de Otero," *Alaluz, Revista de poesía y narración*, 12, 1 (Primavera 1980), p. 80.

Essays

"Review of *León Felipe, poeta de barro*, by Luis Rius." *Books Abroad*, 43, 2 (Spring 1969), pp. 238-39.

"La ideología del hombre en la obra poética de León Felipe." *DAI*, 30, 7 (January 1970), pp. 3021-22A.

"Into the Labyrinth: The Chicano in Literature," *New Voices in Literature: The Mexican-American*. Ed. Edward Simmen, Pan American University, Edinburg, Texas, 1971, pp. 18-25.
[Reprint in *Southwestern American Literature*, 2, 2 (Fall 1972), pp. 90-97.]
[Also presented as paper at Conference on Chicano Literature, Pan American University, October 1971.]

"Literatura chicana: Vida en busca de forma," Paper presented at AATSP, Chicago, December 28-30, 1971.
[Also presented as "Life in Search of Form" at Texas Tech. University Comparative Literature Symposium, Lubbock, Texas, January 28, 1976.]

"Perspectives on Chicano Literature." *Sociological Abstracts*, Special Issue. (Spring 1972), n.p.

"Perspectives: Chicano Literature," Paper presented at MLA, December 1973.

"Chicano Literature: Fiesta of the Living," *Books Abroad/An International Literary Quarterly*, 49, 3 (Summer 1975), pp. 439-52.
[Reprint in *The Identification and Analysis of Chicano Literature*. Ed. Francisco Jiménez, Bilingual Press, Jamaica, New York, 1979, pp. 19-36.]
[Also presented as paper at University of Oklahoma Symposium on Chicano Literature, October 11-12, 1974.]

"La teoría poética de León Felipe," *Cuadernos Americanos*, 186, 1 (January-February 1973), pp. 193-214.

"El idioma español en los EE. UU. de Norteamérica," *Sembradores de Amistad*, 30, 286 (August 1975), pp. 8-11.

"Recuerdo, descubrimiento y voluntad en el proceso imaginativo literario," *Atisbos*. Trans. Gustavo Valadez, No. 1 (Summer 1975), pp. 66-77.
[Reprint in *La Raza Habla*, New Mexico State University, 1, 1 (January 1976), pp. 13-16.]
[Also presented as paper at Indiana University Symposium on ". . . y no se lo tragó la tierra," April 6-7, 1972, and at Merritt College Chicano Writers' Workshop, Oakland, California, June 2, 1973.]
[Also to be published in *Tomás Rivera y la literatura chicana*. Ed. Luis Dávila, Indiana University Publications, Bloomington, Indiana, Chicano-Riqueño Studies, No. 1.]

"We Are All Immigrants," *Express News*, San Antonio, Texas, September 7, 1975, pp. 5H ff.

"Biculturalismo y estructura creativa como emancipación intelectual." Paper presented at MLA Minority Commission, Dallas, Texas, October 1976.

"Dynamic Intimacy in Chicano Literature." Paper presented at MLA, San Francisco, December 1975.
[Also to be published as "Chicano Literature: A Dynamic Intimacy," in Pan American University monograph series, 15 pp.]

"Remarks on Affirmative Action: How do you do?" *El Cuaderno* (TACHE), Vol. 1 (Spring 1977), pp. 9-13.

"On Chicano Literature," *Texas Books in Review*, 1, 1 (1977), pp. 5-6.

"Preface," *Pegasus 77*, San Antonio Public Library, San Antonio, Texas, 1977.

"The Great Plains as a Refuge in Chicano Literature." Paper presented at University of Nebraska, Lincoln, Symposium on Ethnicity on the Great Plains, April 6-7, 1978.
[To be published in 1982 in *Vision and Refuge: Essays on the Literature of the Great Plains*, eds. Virginia Faulkner and Frederick C. Luebke, University of Nebraska Press, Lincoln, Nebraska, 25 pp.]

"Review of *Pensamientos capturados*, by José Montalvo," *Caracol*, 4, 9 (May 1978), n.p.

"The Writings of Hinojosa-Smith: Integrity." To be published in *El Cuaderno* (TACHE), Vol. 2.

"Chicano Literature: The Establishment of Community." Paper presented at Chicano Literature Roundtable, University of California, Santa Barbara, 1979.
[Published in *A Decade of Chicano Literature (1970-79)*, eds. L. Leal, F. de Necochea, F. Lomelí, R. G. Trujillo, Editorial La Causa, Santa Barbara, California, 1982.]

"The Role of the Chicano Academic and the Chicano Non-Academic Community," *Proceedings of the Invitational Symposium, Hispanics in Higher Education: Leadership and Vision for the Next Twenty-five Years*, April 29-May 1, 1982 (paper presented at the University of Texas at Austin).

"The Meaning of Going to College," *Caminos Magazine*, June 1983 (one of several articles), Tomás Rivera, Special Editor.

"Mexican-American Literature: The Establishment of Community," *La Chispa '83: Selected Proceedings*, ed. Gilbert Paolini (paper presented at Louisiana Conference on Hispanic Languages and Literatures, Tulane University, February 10-12, 1983; also presented at the Texas Literary Tradition Conference, University of Texas at Austin, 1983).

Joint Publications

"Mexican American Literature," *The Spanish Speaking American Challenge: A Report on the 1974 BYU Chicano Conference* (T. Rivera, moderator, with Russell Cluff, Merlin Compton, Ted Lyon, and Elaine Miller). Eds. L. Sid Shreeve and Merwin G. Fairbanks, Brigham Young University Latin American Studies, Provo, Utah, 1975, pp. 104-15.

A Public Trust: The Report of the Carnegie Commission on the Future of Public Broadcasting (by Carnegie Commission on the Future of Public Broadcasting—T. Rivera, member), Bantam Books, New York, 1979, 401 pp.

A National Agenda for the Eighties: Report of the President's Commission for a National Agenda for the Eighties (by the Commission—T. Rivera, Member), U.S. Government Printing Office, Washington, D.C. 20402, 1980.

High School—A Report on Secondary Education in America (by the Carnegie Foundation for the Advancement of Teaching High School Panel—T. Rivera, member), Harper & Row, New York, 1983.

TOMAS RIVERA (1935-1984)

Rolando Hinojosa

In the long listing of Tomás Rivera's employment record, in his various vitae, the academic year 1957-1958 shows him as a secondary school English teacher for the Edgewood Independent School District in San Antonio. From there, upward, one reads and finds the last entry, 7/79 to Present: Chancellor, University of California, Riverside. This entry is followed by a parenthesis.

The parenthetical addition was Tomás's own, and he insisted on it, for he considered himself primarily—and quite rightly, of course—a professor, one who professes a subject matter in a classroom. Indeed, in 1983 he conducted a literature class for a number of senior graduate students.

As impressive as the employment record is—and it is that, make no mistake—there is an important entry prior to his Edgewood year of 1957-58: "Up to the time I started my teaching career, I was part of the migrant labor stream that went from Texas to various parts of the Midwest. I lived and worked in Iowa, Minnesota, Wisconsin, Michigan, and North Dakota."

As anyone can see, this man who served as a corporate officer for the Times Mirror Company, as the Executive Vice President and Acting Vice President for Academic Affairs at the University of Texas at El Paso, and who held other administrative posts did not, not once or ever, to my full knowledge, forget who he was, his place of origin, or his past.

I shouldn't want for anyone reading this to think that Tomás boasted about his migratory life; to him, it was merely the work he had done alongside his parents, Don Florencio Rivera and Doña Josefa Hernández de Rivera; something that provided them a hard living, and, ultimately, a reminder that, educationally and socially, there remained much work to be done for many youngsters from a similar background.

The entry, also, pointed to Tomás's manner of facing life squarely, unflinchingly; eye to eye, as it were. He wasn't ashamed of his background, obviously, but then, neither did he attempt to profit, in any way, by its inclusion in his vitae. It was something that had been an active part of his life, and, as such, it was also part of the many lives he had led as an adolescent, in young manhood, as husband, father, friend, and professional.

The harsh working conditions were endured easily enough, he'd say, but it was the deaths of relatives, the waste of latent talents, as well as the lack of educational opportunities for many of his contemporaries that influenced him to a high degree during his lifetime.

Simply put, it was this influential experience that both drove and directed him to improve the lot of the generation that preceded him and the subsequent ones, as well.

And it's no secret either that the migrant life also served as the basis for his "... *y no se lo tragó la tierra*" as well as for some of the other published work, poetry and prose pieces, such as *On The Road to Texas: Pete Fonseca, Eva y Daniel,* and *La cara en el espejo.* The point of all this is that Tomás was not haunted by his past; he didn't live in the past. Those who do, of course, are neurotics, and whatever failings Tomás Rivera had—an impatience at the incompetence of those who passed themselves off as indispensable, for one, and a patent disgust with those who wasted their talent, for another—Tomás Rivera, no neurotic, lived in the present, and he lived it fully.

He also knew how to enjoy himself, and I can't find anyone who could touch Tomás and Concha Rivera as party hosts. It was their house, but it was also yours and gladly. Hard workers both of them, each in a personal way, but people who loved each other as much as they loved life. A solid partnership, and because of it, Tomás's personal and professional lives were easily fused.

A few weeks ago I was working on an introduction for Ron Arias's newest book (a collection of short stories for Arte Público Press) and what set me off in the writing of it was a set of photographs: they show Ron, Tomás, and me at Ron's house in Claremont. It was a happy time, as happy as all my memories of Tomás are: at work, at play, at some long, perhaps prolonged, meeting or other, at our countless readings in schools and universities and people's homes, and in all manner of professional meetings.

In the vita here published, you won't be able to see Tomás's genuine and friendly smile, or know of his fondness for listening to and for telling stories, or of his vision of the world; you will, however, see his capacity for work, his selflessness, and his worldly accomplishments.

In one sense, the reader of these lines and the present writer will never know just how many students and captains of industry Tomás Rivera influenced, helped, guided, and educated. One can certainly guess, but here's something of Tomás's from *Pete Fonseca* that explains part of his life: Uno nunca sabe para quién trabaja.

How true! But Tomás, at the least, had an inkling as well as good knowledge of those he worked for directly. Indirectly is something else, and the irony—and Tomás loved irony—is that those he helped will never know who it was that helped them. This last, by the way, is the first precept by Maimonides in *The Ways of Giving*.

But, as Tomás, would say, "No importa, h'mbre. La cosa es trabajar."

Yes, that too was true: The thing to do was to work. It was at these times that I would quote my father: Better to work for something than for someone; preferible es trabajar para algo y no para alguien.

He believed in this so strongly that he drove himself without quarter, and he also goaded many of us to do better than what we thought we could do. A bit of a convoluted sentence there but he did set a high example by deed not by word, as is the usual case with many of our friends and acquaintances.

It isn't a long piece this one, but it's not meant to be either long or about me; it's about Tomás Rivera, a native son of Crystal City, Texas, who—as the great Manolete—when he couldn't give us anymore, he gave us everything, himself.

UNIVERSITY OF TEXAS, AUSTIN

IV. *In Memoriam*

THE REGENTS OF THE UNIVERSITY OF CALIFORNIA

In Memory of

TOMÁS RIVERA

WHEREAS, the Regents are deeply saddened to learn of the tragic death on May 16 of Tomás Rivera, Chancellor of the Riverside campus since 1979, and a nationally recognized teacher and administrator who truly left a unique imprint on the University and on higher education; and

WHEREAS, because of his extraordinary national reputation as an educator and administrator, Dr. Rivera was named UC Riverside's fourth Chancellor in July 1979, becoming the youngest chief executive in the nine-campus system; and

WHEREAS, Tomás Rivera was that combination of gifted teacher, consummate administrator, and acclaimed poet who brought new dimensions of creativity and vision to his leadership of the Riverside campus; the close ties he forged so carefully between campus and community brought him enduring respect and admiration; in addition, his was a strong voice in both the nation and the community in recognizing that our youth is a resource beyond measure; and

WHEREAS, he served on many distinguished advisory committees, including the Carnegie Foundation for the Advancement of Teaching, the American Association for Higher Education, the American Council on Education, the President's Commission on a National Agenda for the '80s, and most recently the National Commission on Secondary Schooling for Hispanics; and

WHEREAS, in recognition of his contributions and achievements, he received many honors and awards, including recognition from the Chicano News Media Association for outstanding achievements and contributions to the Chicano community, and an award from the Riverside chapter of the National Association for the Advancement of Colored People for demonstrated leadership on the Riverside campus; and

WHEREAS, as a poet, novelist, and literary critic he had many works published in journals and anthologies, was the author of two critically acclaimed books, and contributed to a 1979 Carnegie Commission report titled "Public Trust"; and

WHEREAS, after earning degrees through his doctorate in education, educational administration, Spanish literature, and Romance Languages and Literature, Dr. Rivera taught English and Spanish in secondary schools in Texas and subsequently embarked on his career as a teacher, counselor, director of language laboratories, and lecturer prior to his appointment in 1971 as Director of the Division of Foreign Languages, Literature and Linguistics at the University of Texas, San Antonio, and subsequent appointment as Executive Vice President and Acting Vice President for Academic Affairs at the University of Texas, El Paso; and

WHEREAS, throughout a lifetime of unselfish service and rich productivity, Tomás Rivera embodied the search for excellence and high achievement, a man whose concern, enthusiasm, warmth, and humor touched all who knew him in ways that enlivened and illuminated their lives; a man who gave meaning to the events of the world around him and made that world a finer and more enlightened place;

NOW, THEREFORE, BE IT RESOLVED that the Regents express the deep sense of bereavement which they and the rest of the University community have sustained in the loss of Tomás Rivera, a warm friend and valued colleague, who will be profoundly missed and long remembered;

AND BE IT FURTHER RESOLVED that the Regents convey to Mrs. Rivera and her family their most heartfelt sympathy, and direct that suitably inscribed copies of this resolution be sent to them as a token of the Regents' affection, admiration, and regard for a close and treasured friend.

May 1984

ATTEST:

Bonnie M. Smotony

Secretary of The Regents
of the University of California

HISPANIC HIGHER EDUCATION COALITION TWENTY "F" STREET, N.W. SUITE 108 WASHINGTON, D.C. 20001

(202) 638-7339

May 18, 1984

Mrs. Concepcion Rivera and Family
4171 Watkins Drive
Riverside, California 92507

Dear Mrs. Rivera:

On behalf of the Hispanic Higher Education I want to express most sincere condolences to you and your family. The sudden loss of any loved one is always a jarring and heartfelt shock. The personal impact of Tomás Rivera passing on though is truly of a magnitude that far exceeds anything in recent memory.

Tomás has occupied a singular position in the constellation of Chicano leadership notable by his unique and irreplaceable brand of humanism and dedication to duty. His unflagging role in promoting the equitable access into postsecondary education of Hispanic students and supporting their academic development has served our community well. His commitment to the promotion of Hispanic culture and his contributions to Chicano literature in particular have been worthy of much praise and admiration. Tomás, the man of tempered strength and tremandous integrity, will be missed sorely by those of us honored to have known him.

We will all treasure our memories of Tomás and seek his high visions of a better future for our community. We are much enriched by his glowing legacy.

Respectfully,

Rafael J. Magallan
Executive Director

ASPIRA of America • El Congreso Nacional de Asuntos Colegiales • Latino Institute • League of United American Citizens
Mexican American Legal Defense and Educational Fund • Mexican American Women's National Association
National Association for Equal Education Opportunities • National Council of La Raza • National IMAGE, Inc.
Puerto Rican Legal Defense and Education Fund, Inc. • Secretariat for Hispanic Affairs, U.S. Catholic Conference
Society of Hispanic Professional Engineers • Spanish American League Against Discrimination

LEGISLATIVE ADDRESS
STATE CAPITOL—ROOM 2082
SACRAMENTO, CA 95814
(916) 445-6868

DISTRICT OFFICE ADDRESSES
515 N. ARROWHEAD AVENUE, XXX
SUITE 100
SAN BERNARDINO, CA 92401
(714) 884-3165

2545 SO. EUCLID AVENUE
ONTARIO, CA 91761
(714) 983-3566

Senate

California Legislature

RUBEN S. AYALA
SENATOR

CHAIRMAN
AGRICULTURE AND WATER RESOURCES COMMITTEE

COMMITTEES
AGRICULTURE AND WATER
RESOURCES
ENERGY AND PUBLIC UTILITIES
LOCAL GOVERNMENT
REVENUE AND TAXATION
SELECT COMMITTEE ON CHILDREN
AND YOUTH
JOINT LEGISLATIVE AUDIT
COMMITTEE
SUBCOMMITTEE ON MOBILEHOME
PARK PROBLEMS

May 22, 1984

Mrs. Concepción Rivera and Family
4171 Watkins Drive
Riverside, CA 92507

Dear Mrs. Rivera and Family:

Mrs. Ayala and I were very saddened to learn of the untimely passing of your beloved husband and father, Dr. Tom Rivera, recently.

Dr. Rivera was a highly respected and admired Professional in the Field of Education. You may be assured he will be greatly missed by all who held him in high esteem and, although words seldom relay the deep sympathy one feels toward another upon the loss of a loved one, perhaps the knowledge that your friends' thoughts are with you will help sustain you in the days ahead.

In deep sympathy,

RUBEN S. AYALA
Senator, 34th District

RSA:mer

ESTEBAN E. TORRES
34TH DISTRICT, CALIFORNIA

COMMITTEES:

BANKING, FINANCE AND
URBAN AFFAIRS

SMALL BUSINESS

WASHINGTON OFFICE:
1740 LONGWORTH HOUSE OFFICE BUILDING
WASHINGTON, D.C. 20515
(202) 225–5256

DISTRICT OFFICES:

SADDLEBACK SQUARE
12440 FIRESTONE BLVD.
SUITE 117
NORWALK, CALIFORNIA 90650
(213) 929–2711

HOME FEDERAL SAVINGS & LOAN BLDG.
1400 WEST COVINA PARKWAY
SUITE 201
WEST COVINA, CALIFORNIA 91790
(213) 814–1557

Congress of the United States
House of Representatives
Washington, D.C. 20515

June 1, 1984

Concepcion Rivera and Family
4171 Watkins Drive
Riverside, California   92507

Dear Mrs. Rivera:

On behalf on myself and my wife Arcy, I would like to
express my most sincere condolences to you and your family.

Tomas Rivera was an individual who gave much to our
community and he will be missed. His long record of
promoting the just development of Chicano students and
Chicano leadership in higher education speaks for itself.
His literary works promoted Hispanic culture at the highest
levels. I enjoyed Tomas' novel and his poetry and feel that
he communicated directly to the hearts of all.

I think of Tomas principally as the archetype of, "un hombre
educado," a man of learning with an unimpeachable sense of
honor, respectful of others, high integrity, quiet resolve
and a commitment to social justice. His unflagging efforts
on behalf of all Chicanos shall serve as a truly
inspirational model.

If I can be of service to you during these difficult days,
please call on me.

Sincerely,

Esteban E. Torres
Member of Congress

LLOYD BENTSEN
TEXAS

COMMITTEES:
FINANCE
ENVIRONMENT AND PUBLIC WORKS
JOINT ECONOMIC
SELECT COMMITTEE
ON INTELLIGENCE
JOINT COMMITTEE
ON TAXATION

United States Senate

WASHINGTON, D.C. 20510

June 19, 1984

Mrs. Concepcion Rivera
4171 Watkins Drive
Riverside, California   92507

Dear Mrs. Rivera:

I was saddened to learn of the death of your husband. With
his passing, we have lost a distinguished educator and one
of our great leaders. He has touched the lives of many and
will be sorely missed.

I have enclosed a copy of a statement I read into the
Congressional Record in memory of your late husband.

B.A. joins me in extending our sincerest sympathies to you
and your family.

Sincerely,

Lloyd Bentsen

Lloyd Bentsen

BURCIAGA ·85
I

TOMÁS RIVERA...Y NO SE LO TRAGÓ LA TIERRA

BORCIAGA 85
III

TOMAS RIVERA, 1935-1984
SO PROUD OF YOU FOREVER

James H. Abbott

Dr. Tomás Rivera, whose death on May 16, 1984, ended an ever-ascending series of accomplishments, was the first member of a minority group to ever be appointed chancellor in the University of California system. He was also the youngest, 43, at the time of his appointment to this position for which he was nominated without having applied. Rivera began his academic career as a high school teacher in Texas in 1957, and after progressing through the academic hierarchy to the chancellorship at the University of California, Riverside, he stated in an interview that his ultimate goal was to return to the classroom. This goal was reached in a way he had not envisioned, for simultaneously with his other accomplishments, he had established a reputation as a prize-winning creative writer in both Spanish and English. Wherever Chicano literature is studied, Tomás Rivera will always be in the classroom.

A list of achievements tells only facts about a man whose personal qualities set him apart from other men. Rivera, who began his life in Crystal City, Texas, the son of migrant workers, knew firsthand the hardships and prejudices inflicted on his people. For a nickel a day, he studied in Spanish-speaking *barrio* schools as well as in public schools throughout the Midwest, wherever necessity led his family. His parents, Florencio and Josefa Hernández Rivera, instilled in him a love of reading and a belief in strong family ties, both of which were evident throughout his life.

After high school in Crystal City, Rivera earned degrees at Southwest Texas Junior College. Southwest Texas State Collge, and at the University of Oklahoma, where in 1969 he completed an M.A. in Spanish and a Ph.D. with a major in Spanish and a minor in French. Because of his recognizably outstanding qualities, a friend of his had recommended that Dr. Lowell Dunham, then chairman of the department of modern languages, offer him a graduate assistantship, and after Rivera had completed his graduate courses, the chairman asked him to supervise student teachers in foreign languages.

From the University of Oklahoma, Rivera moved with extraordinary ease and rapidity to positions as professor of Spanish at Sam Houston State University and the University of Texas at San Antonio, where he later became dean of the College of Multi-disciplinary Studies, then vice president. At San Antonio he was a key force in the organization of the curriculum for the opening of that new university. Immediately prior to his appointment at the University of California, Riverside, Rivera was vice president of the University of Texas at El Paso.

The man who accomplished so much in a relatively short time attracted opportunities for success because of what he was and because his ideals and his abilities were apparent in all situations: professional, familial, social and creative. Rivera was a man who, like Don Quixote, knew who he was. He built on his past and projected himself dynamically into the future with a great human sentiment and a constant sense of humor, never hesitant to manifest either of them.

In his professional life he made decisions based on substantial knowledge of each situation but always without undue delay. His self-knowledge and confidence led him to be impatient with cumbersome committees, although he always adhered to democratic processes. When faced with difficult problems and decisions, he remembered the Spanish proverb, "a mal paso, dale prisa" (when you have something bad to do, hurry up and do it); he disliked leaving important issues unresolved.

His decisions were based on his belief in quality education for everybody, but he was especially sensitive to minority needs. At times Rivera was concerned that media attention to his own background might create a caricature or stereotype. He preferred to be accepted, not because he was a Chicano, but because of his own qualifications and his qualities as a human being. He found such an acceptance in many places, but especially at the University of Oklahoma. When he dedicated a copy of his prize-winning work, "... *y no se lo tragó la tierra/And the Earth Did Not Part*, to Dr. and Mrs. Lowell Dunham, he wrote, "quienes me han recibido como persona y como amigo. El profesor Dunham . . . siempre me ha humanizado las cosas" (". . . who have always received me as a person and a friend. Professor Dunham . . . has always humanized things for me.")

Rivera also was concerned with Chicano community reactions to his position as a role model and his decisions regarding quality education. Although his own background was an inspiration to him in the creative process, he did not want minorities relegated to a minority world, preferring instead that they be well-educated first and minorities second. This attitude no doubt contributed to his plans to abolish both the program of Chicano Studies and Black Studies at the University of California, Riverside, a decision he made without fear, because he believed that it was the best decision for everybody.

Because he knew himself, Rivera was not afraid to inject his wry humor into any situation, once declaring to a reporter that his only defect was, "I'm fat." Again, during an interview for the University of California, Riverside chancellorship, when a committee member expressed astonishment that Rivera planned to spend only a week studying the University of California system, he replied, "O.K., two weeks." As co-director of the University of Oklahoma Summer Session in Madrid in the 1970s, he began every day with a smile that set the tone for the group and his presence helped create one of the happiest and most productive sessions in the life of the program.

His love of people and his eagerness to help began in his relationship with his own parents, extended to all of humanity, and is nowhere more evident than in his own closely knit family. "The family is the final support group that one has," he once remarked. He and his wife, Concha, in spite of their busy schedules, always made room for at least one meal a day as a family unit, and they made a practice of spending a week's vacation time alone with each of their three children. He and Concha communicated to them a love of reading, a set of moral and social values, and their creative talents. Rivera's succes as a parent is evident in the success of his children. Ileana, a teacher, Irasema, who works in drug rehabilitation, and Javier, a high school senior, exemplify the high personal, social and educational standards that their father wanted for everybody.

Rivera's standards of quality applied to all phases of life, but especially to education. As a student he always was prepared, always cheerful and considered the extensive readings required of graduate students as a part of the habits he already had established. Many of his teachers recognized that his global grasp of concepts and his awareness of the role of his own studies as a fragment of a larger fabric marked him as a thinker and a man capable of acting in a world beyond specialization.

Like Ortega y Gasset's *hombre selecto*, Rivera set his own goals, always demanding more of himself then merely fulfilling requirements established by others. His thoroughness and the quality of his academic interests are evident in his dissertation on León Felipe, a substantial part of which was published in *Cuadernos Hispanoamericanos*. His numerous papers, more than 72 by 1979, attest to his continued interest in scholarly activities. His participation in many symposia on Chicano literature, the first one organized at the University of Oklahoma, kept him in touch with scholars and writers in his field. His activities in that area became international in scope, and he was to have participated in a Chicano literature symposium in Germany in the summer of 1984.

He seemed always to find time, however, for his creative writing, and his first published, "*. . . y no se lo tragó la tierra"/And the Earth Did Not Part*, won the Quinto Sol National Literary Prize in 1970. Other works have appeared in collections such as *Songs and Dreams, El Espejo/The Mirror, Café solo,* and in *Aztlán: An Anthology of Texas Poets,* and *The Chicano Short Story*. He also contributed to professional journals and was a member of the editorial board of MICTLA Publications and *El Magazín,* as well as contributing editor to *El Grito* and *Revista Chicano-Riqueña. Always and Other Poems* was his last volume of poetry, and at the time of his death he was working on a larger volume of poetry and a novel, *The Large House in Town*. His writing ranged from his critical studies of literature to his own literary creations, now themselves the subject of critical works and topics for dissertations on Mexican-American literature. Rivera's works show both his interest in the creative process and his association with the Chicano Community, since his creative production is centered around the Chicano experience.

Although he was always an integral part of the Chicano culture, Rivera never advocated special consideration or favors simply on the basis of minority status. He did not want to become chancellor at University of California, Riverside as a concession, but rather because he was qualified for the position. His attitude about his personal goals represented his hopes for all Chicanos, as well as all of humanity. He accepted responsibilities with the hope that he could somehow improve the human condition, and he was ever optimistic about the possibilities. His appointment to President Carter's Commission on a National Agenda for the 1980s, the Carnegie Foundation for the Advancement of Teaching, the American Association for Higher Education, and the American Council on Education and Educational Testing Services are only a few of the challenges that he met with the same sense of dedication that he showed in his other endeavors. Even with such a great number of demands on his time, he still found energy for visiting elementary schools to encourage children to strive for excellence in their studies to achieve high standards of moral behavior.

In all of his activities, whether as teacher, administrator, father or writer, Rivera never lost sight of the human qualities and the humanitarian values he believed to be essential to all progress and justice. His sense of humor, his self-knowledge and an unlimited love for humanity are only some of the qualities which drew to him the opportunities and challenges he accepted so enthusiastically. He has returned now to the classroom through his writing and the example he set for so many people. His ultimate goal has been reached, and with his burial in Crystal City on May 19, 1984, he has returned to the point where his life began.

Memories of Tomás Rivera will last forever in the history of higher education, as well as in the classroom and in Mexican-American literature. In a letter to Dunham, October 5, 1979, Rivera recalled, with humor and sentiment, the lean years of graduate school and the human qualities he appreciated in others:

"How can I ever thank you and the modern languages faculty enough for the advice, academic preparation and professional ethics that all of you gave me? As I have told you many times, coming out of Texas, looking and feeling as if I had fallen out of a tree (as you would say), I had no idea what waited for Concha, myself and our three kids. What we found in Norman was a group of warm, caring people who were willing to take a chance on us. We grasped every minute, and Concha and I have the fondest memories of you all (as they say in Texas). Concha and I still remember that Thanksgiving Day when we really were down to a couple of dollars (no turkey, no booze, *nada*, except three kids with chicken pox) when out of nowhere you showed up at our door with a couple of bottles of wine and two of the best-tasting loaves of bread (homemade). We were so proud of you forever.''

The University of Oklahoma and everybody who knew Tomás Rivera can make these words their own: ''We were so proud of you forever.''

UNIVERSITY OF OKLAHOMA

REMEMBERING TOMAS RIVERA

Luis Leal

The Chicano academic community suffered a great loss with the passing of Tomás Rivera, Chancellor of the University of California, Riverside, last May sixteenth. His illnes and unexpected death left us with great sadness. Tomás represented the fulfillment of the aspirations of Chicano academics. His career in the academic world has been sensational, for he had been able to conquer the insurmountable obstacles which Chicanos often face.

Tomás Rivera was able to reach the high position he held due to his personal qualities, that is, a great reserve of physical energy, a well-defined goal in life, a great desire to help his fellow men, and an unusual sense of human and social values.

In his poem "The Searchers" we find these significant verses which reveal to us, better than anything else he wrote, his sentiments and his faith in the destiny of man:

> We were not alone
> after many centuries
> How could we be alone
> We searched together
> We were seekers
> We are searchers
> and we will continue
> to search
> because our eyes
> still have
> the passion of prophecy.

I met Tomás Rivera in Guadalajara. Mexico, in 1963, when the future Chancellor was attending a summer Institute for teachers of bilingual education organized by the University of Arizona. Since then, I kept in touch with him and followed very closely his rapid progress in the educational world: receiving his doctorate in Oklahoma in 1969; teaching at Sam Houston University from 1969 to 1971; becoming a Dean and later Vice-President at the University of Texas, in San Antonio; holding the position of Executive President at the University of Texas, El Paso; and, finally, becoming the first member of a minority, in 1979, to be appointed to the position of Chancellor of one of the branches of the University of California. His early death five years later prevented him from developing the well-thought-out program he had envisioned for the University, especially the establishment of a research center dedicated to the study of United States-Mexico relations. If such a center is established, we hope it is given the name of Tomás Rivera as a remembrance of his efforts in that endeavor.

Rivera's administrative ability and his great concern for the educational problems of minority students earned him several honors, being named a member of the board of the Carnegie Foundation for the Advancement of Teaching, receiving a presidential appointment to the Board of Foreign Scholarships which directs and administers the Fulbright program, and being named a member of the board of the National Chicano Council on Higher Education. In 1980 he served on the presidential commission established with the purpose of identifying the educational problems that the nation will face during the eighties. In spite of having attained all these honors, Tomás never changed, never stopped being the same person I had met in 1963, when he was an unknown high school teacher in a Texas town. He was always affable, always ready to extend a hand when needed, always defending the rights of the minority student.

Besides his public life as the administrator of one of the campuses of the prestigious University of California, Rivera was also well known in literary circles as a writer of prose and poetry. Although he published only two books and a few articles—his second novel, La casa grande, has never been published—he was able to influence greatly the trend that Chicano literature was to take during the seventies. His most important work is, of course, "...And the Earth Did Not Part," a novel composed of short narratives which was awarded the Premio Quinto Sol in 1970 and published in 1971. This work has been thoroughly examined by literary critics, all of them having expressed nothing but praise, either for its original structure, its terse style, or its faithful presentation of Chicano life. Less well known is his collection *Always and Other Poems*, where we find, as in his prose, the same optimistic attitude towards life, and the same faith in the future of the Chicano community.

Another activity which attracted Rivera, as a writer, was literary criticism. His studies of Chicano literature mark a well-defined belief in the social function of literature. By reading his essays on literature we come to the conclusion that he firmly believed that the principal function of Chicano literature is the creation of a sense of community.

In literature written by his own people, he tells us, the Chicano finds that he can identify with the characters, the ideas and beliefs, and the experiences narrated, that is, with the culture that those works document. Thus, by reading works written by Chicanos, the Chicano reader can reinforce the ties that bind him to his own community and which give him a sense of identity. All Chicano writers, Rivera tells us, write about things that the Chicano reader is intimately acquainted with, and not about things he has learned. By selecting materials found in the community, the Chicano writer can give his own reality a form, a form that previously had been denied to it.

With his slender books, Tomás Rivera has greatly helped to show the way in which it is possible to give a form to the reality experienced by the Chicano. At the same time, he has fulfilled another of the missions pointed out in his articles, that of preserving and transmitting Chicano culture to future generations. This should not lead us to believe that he was parochial in his attitude towards literature, for, as he said in one of his essays, literature can, "by drawing upon cultural origins, provide a perception of the world, of people, of ourselves in awe of one's own life and its perplexities, its complexities and its beauty."

Tomás Rivera's early death did not permit him to finish his second novel, with which we are sure he would have advanced his ardent desire to give form to Chicano reality. His life, although short, was exemplary and will serve as an inspiration to all of us to carry on his work to search for and preserve Chicano culture in all its forms.

UNIVERSITY OF CALIFORNIA, SANTA BARBARA

TOMAS RIVERA: THE CREATION OF THE
CHICANO EXPERIENCE IN FICTION

Alfonso Rodríguez

In this paper I would like to express a few thoughts on Tomás Rivera, the man and his fiction, and on the community where he and I spent our formative years. The same community from which he drew inspiration to write his novel "*. . . y no se lo tragó la tierra.*" As I fuse remembrance, experience and testimony I would like to pay a small tribute to his memory.

As one who sees his experience and that of his family, friends and neighbors reflected in Rivera's work, I derive a great deal of meaning by returning to a certain time, a certain space, to take stock of our circumstances and try to understand what our reality consists of; where we were and where we have gone, as individuals, and as a people.

As I reflect on these things I pose the question: What, then, is the Chicano experience? Other people on the face of the earth experience economic oppression, racial discrimination, tragedy and death, the crippling effects of superstition, but also a genuine contact with the realm of the sacred, the tyranny of time, cultural alienation, discord within their own community, a burning desire for self expression, a need to break out of the cycle of poverty and complacency, hope in the midst of devastating circumstances, and so forth. The only conclusion that I reach is that, as Chicanos, we experience all these things in a slightly different way from other people, insofar as our experience is always clothed in its own peculiar modalities. And that is what makes our history unique.

This uniqueness was captured by Tomás in his fiction with simple eloquence and authenticity, creating a narrative structure that immediately placed the Chicano novel in the mainstream of American letters.

Tomás Rivera was born in Crystal City, Texas, in 1935. Prior to 1963, few people outside the Winter Garden District, where Crystal City is located, had any notion of the existence of the place. Then, all of a sudden, it was catapulted into the national limelight when it became the hottest spot in Texas politics.

For many years Crystal City has maintained a population of slightly less than 10,000. It is the seat of Zavala County, named after Lorenzo de Zavala, the 19th century Mexican liberal who rebelled against Santa Anna and the conservative system of government by joining the cause for Texas independence; and later in 1836, he became the first vice-president of the Republic of Texas. It seems that many mexicanos on both sides of the border still see him as a traitor. However, the overwhelming majority of mexicanos in Crystal City have not the remotest idea who Lorenzo de Zavala was; at the mention of his name one notices an attitude similar to the one seen in the two women with repect to the state of Utah in the introductory vignette to the story "Es que duele" in *Tierra*. One seriously doubts the existence of such a place, the other speculates that if, indeed, it exists it must be very close to Japan.

To local Chicanos, Crystal City is known as Cristal or "El Vidrio." Cattle ranching and agriculture are the main industries in the area. During the fifties and early sixties, Chicanos made up around 80 percent of the voting population. Yet the city government and the school board were in the hands of the Anglo minority. Up to 1963, Mr. Wholesomeback had served as mayor of the city for 38 consecutive years. Then things exploded, marking a turning point in the city's history, and nothing has ever been the same again. Five Chicanos took control of the local government in an unprecedented political victory. Once a commitment was made to obtain representation in government there was no turning back.

The five candidates exhibited an unusual amount of courage in the midst of abuse against them and their families, loss of jobs for some of them, and death threats against all. The Chicanos won the election due to a well-organized campaign and because the people came out of their indifference and delivered the votes. There was an interesting maneuver on the part of the Anglos, a last desperate attempt to hold on to the reins of power. Many of them who had been resting in their graves for more than five years tried to excercise the right to vote *in absentia*; but that attempt was not fruitful.

There are great lessons to be learned from what occurred in 1963. Today after years of turmoil, Chicanos and Anglos in Crystal City see each other as equals and there is a remarkable degree of social harmony. Both communities take pride in the fact that Crystal City, for many many years, has enjoyed the reputation of being the "Spinach Capital of the World," at least in that area. Both communities get together to plan and organize the Spinach Festival, a recent event which has been celebrated three years in a row.

On the south side of City Hall there is a huge statue of Popeye which stands as the symbol of the source of Anglo inspiration and contribution to knowledge and culture. On the west side of the same building one can see the bronze, taciturn figure of Don Benito Juárez and his famous dictum inscribed on a wall: "Entre los individuos como entre las naciones, el respeto al derecho ajeno es la paz." Since the late sixties, the image of Juárez has been a source of inspiration for local Chicanos, who have been struggling to make Crystal City a decent place to live.

I have thought of the first framework story in *Tierra*, "El año perdido," in relation to events in Crystal City around 1963. Like the boy-hero in the story, the people had been trapped in a recurring cycle, a cycle of unawareness of our own singularity, a cycle of alienation from each other, a cycle of frustration and impotence. But in 1963, the people heard the voice of our collective unconscious and the cycle was broken, marking the beginning of the beginning of a new experience. Of course, "El año perdido" can be interpreted in several different ways, but as I consider the Chicano experience in Tomás's fiction, I focus on the particular and the universal becomes more apparent.

My family and I moved to Crystal City from northern Coahuila (just across the Río Bravo) in June of 1954. By a design of destiny, or perhaps by an act of Providence, we ended up at 307 Valverde Street, not far from the Rivera household, which was, and still is, located at 513 Valverde, right on the edge of Mexico Viejo, on the west side of town; a low area which experiences floods from time to time. Tomás's father and mine met in the fields of the Winter Garden District doing piece work (clipping onions in the spring and cutting spinach in the winter), or at times, working for 45 cents an hour in the sorghum fields. The hopes, dreams, trials and tribulations of Chicano field hands, both in Texas and in the northern states as migrant workers, are beautifully portrayed in stories such as "Los niños no se aguantaron," "Y no se lo tragó la tierra," "Los quemaditos," and "Cuando lleguemos." In these stories Tomás writes about his own experience and the experience of a hard working, long suffering people who exhibit a quiet stoicism in their daily life, but also a spirit of rebellion against injustice.

Because of our difference in age, Tomás and I belonged to different groups. To me, Tomás and his younger brother Henry were simply Tony's older brothers, nothing more. Tony (who is now a physician in "El Centro de Salud" in Crystal City) and I are about the same age. We became very good friends. We were in the same class in school, we both played football and baseball, and each, in his own way, in his own time, assimilated influence from Tomás.

During the late fifties and early sixties we acquired a bicultural education of sorts outside the classroom. We would go to "El Teatro Luna" and "El Teatro Alameda" to see movies of Pedro Infante, Jorge Negrete, Cantinflas, Lalo González (El Piporro), Sara García, Prudencia Grifell, María Félix, Arturo de Córdova, Marga López, Tin Tan y su carnal Marcelo, Tongolele, María Antonieta Pons, Andrés Soler, Manolín y Chilinski, Clavillazo, Resortes and many more. We felt completely at home in this atmosphere. However, at the Guild Theater, it was a different story. The environment there was cold, even hostile for many of us, especially those that were not assimilated. Experiences like the one described in the vignette preceding the story "La noche estaba plateada" in *Tierra* were not uncommon. After he is denied service at the barber shop the little boy "crossed the street, and waited around for the theater to open, but then the barber came outside and told him to get away from there. Everything was then perfectly clear, and he went home to get his father." (p. 37) Each experience that we had similar to this one, made us more and more stubborn. As we used to say in those days: "Nos hacíamos más conchudos." At first, we would suppress anxiety and feelings of rejection, and then, in time, we learned to overcome all fear. Our concern was to gain access into the theater to see cowboys and Indians, Roy Rogers, Gene Autry, Cisco Kid and Pancho, Tarzan, James Dean, Marlon Brando; and later, Elvis movies, after we had been infected by the bug of rock and roll.

At home, with our parents, we would listen to Mexican music: rancheras by José Alfredo Jiménez or Lola Beltrán; boleros by el Trío Los Panchos, Toña la Negra or Agustín Lara; norteñas with acordeón and bajo sexto; or conjunto music from El Valle. But as soon as we had an opportunity we tuned in to KTSA in San Antonio to listen to the latest rock and roll hits.

We called ourselves "mexicanos," but in the presence of Anglos we were Mexican Americans. There were, however, a few middle class mexicanos who saw themselves as Latin Americans, although no one understood what that meant. In 1963, when the political volcano erupted, the Latin Americans gave their wholehearted support to the opposition thinking that the mexicanos did not stand a chance due to their lack of political experience or perhaps because their uncouth way of doing things. Some Latin Americans became outcasts in their own community when one of them declared publicly that he did not have a drop of Mexican blood flowing through his veins, although, externally, he bore a striking resemblance to "El Indio Fernández." This attitude of self-denigration was caused, in part, by a tremendous pressure to conform to a different system of cultural values. There were dense vestiges of social Darwinism floating in the air.

In 1958, Tomás returned to Crystal City from Southwest Texas State College to become our eighth grade general science teacher at Sterling H. Fly Junior High School. Mr. Logan, who had been our regular teacher since the beginning of the school year, resigned at midterm to return to college to begin a graduate program. No one in class, with the exception of Tony, knew who Mr. Logan's replacement was going to be. We were struck with awe and astonishment when Tomás walked into the classroom and pronounced words to this effect: "Beginning today I will be your science teacher." Up to that point we had not had a Chicano for a teacher. It was always a Mr. Moore, Miss Savage, Mr. Ray, Miss Courtney, Mr. Marburger; but never a Spanish surname. Initially, neither Anglos nor mexicanos could conceive the idea of having Tomás as our regular science teacher. We became noisy and unruly, but we were immediately subdued by him. We were all so accustomed to seeing Chicano bus drivers, janitors, or cooks in the school cafeteria. But a Chicano teacher was unheard of. The Chicano students in class were a homogeneous group in terms of social class. All, without exception, were children of migrant families. The Anglos constituted a mixed group. A few were poor, especially those with Polish names; most were of lower middle class background and the rest were the offspring of the power brokers in town. Tomás, with professional seriousness, tempered by that friendly smile that never left him, soon won the respect of everyone and the admiration of many.

Tomás was a trailblazer who made it easier for his students to work toward the fulfillment of their goals. Because of the trust our parents placed in us and their constant encouragement we felt we had to find a way to break away from our condition of migratory laborers; not that there is any indignity in doing that type of work. But our parents had other plans for us. They were convinced that we could forge a better future for ourselves since we had an opportunity that they did not have when they were our age. They were willing to make the ultimate sacrifice for us. And they persevered. Tomás's parents and mine were like the parents of the protagonist in the story "Es que duele." They would not dare face the teacher or the principal on our first day of school or whenever we got in trouble. They felt uncomfortable in the school setting because of the absence of brown faces among teachers and administrators, but their support in other ways never failed. Like the boy's father in the story, they felt a sense of pride in our academic accomplishments and they enjoyed boasting about it to their neighbors and compadres. Some kids already had their life programmed. Their plan consisted of procuring a high school diploma, finding a job at a local establishment such as Willie Lone's Furniture Store, J.C. Penney's or Alamo Lumber Company, getting married and forming a family. In those days a high school diploma was something to be treasured, especially by a Chicano migrant worker. Some kids were not very excited about school, but they had big dreams nonetheless. They dreamed of playing in the major leagues for the Brooklyn Dodgers or for the Cleveland Indians (because Beto Avila, the Mexican star second baseman, played for them). Others dreamed of becoming prize fighters like Raúl Ratón Macías or Sugar Ray Robinson. There is an allusion to this type of dream in the story "Los quemaditos" in *Tierra*. The father envisions the possibility of one of his sons becoming a prize fighter so he can pull the family out of the cycle of poverty. But the story ends in tragedy as his dream becomes a nightmare.

"Los quemaditos" is based on a true story. The specific circumstances were somewhat different, but the pain and the anguish were the same. Around 1961, seven children and their mother burned to death while they slept, leaving behind the father and the oldest son. The fire was caused by an explosion in the furnace. I remember very vividly that most of the Chicano students in high school were excused from classes so we could attend the funeral. At the cemetery there were eight coffins, all of different sizes, lined up beside their graves. The survivors in the family, their relatives and neighbors were beyond consolation.

These tragedies were not uncommon in our community. In fact, Tomás and his family went through an extremely painful experience when his father lost his life in an accident returning home from the spinach fields late one afternoon. This autobiographical incident appears in the vignette that introduces the Christmas story, "La noche buena," in *Tierra*. "La noche buena" is the story that corresponds to the month of December in the lost year the protagonist is recuperating in his memory. Tomás's father died in December of 1959, two weeks before Christmas. Fiction and reality differ on one point only; according to the story, there were sixteen casualties. In real life, there was only one: Don Florencio Rivera.

In his brief stay in Crystal City as a professional, Tomás served as a role model for many of us. No one from his general science class ever made it to the major leagues or took up boxing as a profession, but some eventually developed an interest in a college education and went on to pursue a career. One of his students from that class in 1958 who assimilated Tomás's influence in a remarkable way was Saúl Sánchez, the author of *Hay plesha lichans tu di flac.* He attended the same institutions of higher education as did his former teacher, and majored in the same areas, and eventually completed a Ph.D. Saúl's collection of short stories is based on his own observations and experiences in the mexicano community of Crystal City, but Tomás's influence is unmistakable. It is amazing how a teacher can touch the life of a student simply by setting a good example.

Looking back to the late fifties and early sixties, I now realize that being a Chicano teacher in Crystal City in those years, was like dying a slow, spiritual, painless death, unless one had the moral fortitude to live in constant agony trying to suppress and overcome rejection by the system. Fortunately Tomás left in an opportune moment, and in doing so he made a greater contribution to his community, for in a very real sense he never left Crystal City.

When I read *Tierra* for the very first time, I was a university student learning to analyze literary texts in an objective, cerebral way; without emotion, without intuition. But the impact that Tomás's novel had on me was so overwhelming that by the time I finished reading the second story, I had already discarded all the teachings I had accumulated in my literary theory and stylistics classes, at least for the time being. And as I read story after story I laughed and cried at the same time, because they made me relive a good portion of my experience here on earth, and the experience of other people whose lives had touched mine in one way or another.

I noticed that part of the Chicano experience portrayed in *Tierra* was the variety of Spanish Tomás used to narrate the stories. It was our own dialect, the one teachers and administrators attempted so persistently to eradicate through physical punishment and psychological torture everytime we were caught speaking it. Throughout most of the Southwest, especially the border areas, an essential component of our collective reality is precisely the variety of Spanish, with its diverse characteristics, found in *Tierra*.

At first I did not stop to consider the novel's universal appeal nor the profound insights it expresses about human nature. In the *Introduction* to the first edition, Herminio Ríos makes reference to the value of Ramón and Juanita in the story "La noche que se apagaron las luces" as the archetype of the eternal couple, like Calixto and Melibea, and Romeo and Juliet, whose love always ends in tragedy. However, when I read the story I automatically returned to a Sunday night about ten years before the publication of the novel. It was at the "Salón Campestre" in Crystal City. The famous duet "Los Alegres de Terán" from the state of Nuevo León were playing when all of a sudden, right before intermission time, there was a blackout. Those of us who were at the dance waited and waited for the power to be restored, but to no avail. We found out later that night that someone had attempted suicide by casting himself against one of the transformers in the electric plant, which was located half a block from the dance hall. In *Tierra* the story has a tragic ending; in real life, however, the lover received a tremendous shock, physical and emotional, second degree burns on one side of his face and his right ear shrank to the size of a tiny mushroom.

A few years ago I was invited by the Superintendent of Crystal City Independent School District to give a series of workshops on language and culture to a group of teachers, most of whom are natives of Crystal City. As we read and discussed some of Tomás's stories I was fascinated at the response of the teachers; at the way they approached the stories from their particular perspective as members of the community Tomás had chosen as his frame of reference for writing the novel; at the way they fused fiction and reality by pointing to specific incidents Tomás had incorporated into his literary creation, incidents in which they had been involved either as observers or participants. Like the young protagonist in *Tierra* they were able to recover time in memory in a meaningful way.

In addition to its importance as a social document, *Tierra* is the radiography of a people.

The Chicano experience, in real life and in the novel, is universal. We have all searched for existential and cultural identity. Like the young protagonist in *Tierra*, we have spent time "Under the House," that repository of memory, history and tradition; that dark, closed space like a mother's womb; like the belly of the fish where Jonah spent three days and three nights; like the tomb of Jesus. We have been there in solitude and we have emerged with a sense of renewal and a new vision of the world. And we have discovered that individual destiny is inextricably welded to the destiny of others. This was the experience of Tomás. It was his personal interpretation of Ortega y Gasset's affirmation: "Yo soy yo y mi circunstancia." It has been our experience and the experience of many other human beings.

UNIVERSITY OF NORTHERN COLORADO

DEAR TOMAS

Ron Arias

Stamford, Connecticut

Dear Tomás,

I've written to only one other dead person in my life—my son, who was hit and killed by a car when he was 6-1/2 years old. Writing to him focused my grief; but writing to you is a way of sharing with others a feeling we had in common.

I never felt we had urgent things to say to each other. After I heard that you had died, I felt no regret that I hadn't been able to tell you "just one more thing, one more story." What I regretted deeply was that your own personal story had ended so abrubtly. Yours was the best story of all, better than any of your fictions because these were only a part of you. And there was so much more to you than stories and poems.

In the years we had known each other, we mostly met at parties, receptions, conferences, or at backyard get-togethers at your house or mine. I laughed a lot when I was with you. But you were as good a listener, too, as you were a *cuentero*. Corny as it sounds, we were almost always on the same wave length. I never felt we had to *explain* things to each other. A word, expression, gesture or laugh would do perfectly.

Now and then we would talk literature—works and writers were either good or bad, and that was that. If we said anything else, it would only make us sound like professional critics or academics using lots of long words. I would much rather hear about how you and Rolando had to stand in the *menudo* line Sunday morning holding your pails, along with all the other early-morning errand-runners of the Riverside barrio. I can see you two now, one a university chancellor and the other a professor, both unshaven, in Levis and old shirts—definitely *rasquachi*. Then after getting your *menudo*, you had to go to another place, again to stand in line this time for tortillas.

Not much to say now except that I sorely miss your presence—not you the writer or the chancellor, but you the friend, the guy who made me laugh, the Tomás with that crazy-impish spirit for inventing *a lo mejicano,* just like the narrator of one of your lighter pieces about a savvy drifter named el Pete Fonseca. *Puro pelado.* I'll read it again. At least you left me Pete and a lot of other characters.

Abrazos mil,

Ron

V. Poetry in Memory of Tomás Rivera

CHILDREN'S POEMS

Richard Guel (age 12)

Remembrance of Tomás Rivera

Whenever I step out into the morning breeze
I remember a friend who is now deceased.

He was more than a friend,
he was family to me.
Yet, there was something about him
that made me proud to be just me.

Although I knew him for such a short time,
the last time I saw him I was hoping for another good time.

My feelings were crushed when I heard the sad news,
sadness and grief are nothing new,
but to think it happened to a friend you just knew . . .

As tears roll down my cheeks,
I'm just thinking on how life is so quick.

I will always remember Tomás Rivera
because he had so much to offer . . .

Tomás
Honest thoughtful
Struggled all his life
We all loved him
Rivera

Terrific
Outstanding
Magical
Achieving
Solemn

Paul Silva

Tomás

Sometimes I think of a person I knew
A special kind of person
That only comes
From a few.

He was a great man
For some people
He would take a stand
He was full of courage
And he would create books
That for our brain would nourish.

When I See Him

When I see him
the room is never dim.
I see pride and joy
that is usually seen
in the mind of a young boy.

When I see him, I see faith,
that's what all should sayeth.

I'll see him again, some day
like on that day in May,
But that shall be the day when I
see
the Creator of this world
Oh, what a time that will be!

In memory we shall have
the man we all care of,

the man, Tomás Rivera.

Dear Mrs. Rivera,

I'm sorry to hear about your husband, he was an extraordinary man. It was a great loss to you *and* to us. Except, I know you are as strong as your husband.

You should always look back at the memories you had with him and maybe some words he said you'll remember, this will help you. I hope you will be feeling better soon.

Respectfully yours,

Paul Silva

CORRIDOS AND OTHER POEMS

Héctor P. Márquez

Corrido de Tomás Rivera

Día diez y seis de mayo
la gente se estremeció
pues llegó mala noticia
Tomás Rivera murió.

¿La tierra se lo tragó?
¡La tierra se lo ha tragado!
Sus hazañas vivirán
y nunca será olvidado.

Lejos de Texas andaba
distante su pueblo natal,
llora este pueblo que amaba
llora su madre cabal.

Mucho bien hizo este hombre
a quien tantos conocían
se lució primero en Texas
californios lo aplaudían.

Hizo mucho por su raza
buen maestro y profesor,
fue profesionista astuto,
líder, poeta, y asesor.

Fue primero entre los buenos
un ejemplo para todos,
puente entre los dos países
con los listos codo a codo.

¿Quién olvidará sus cuentos
de los niños quemaditos,
del pícaro Pete Fonseca
Laíto y Bone los malditos;

de los que quieren "llegar"
mas no saben cómo y cuándo,
del que perdió un año entero
del que al diablo anda buscando?

¿Quién olvidará sus versos,
versos del limón partido,
los que con su clara voz
cantó al público cumplido?

Siempre tuvo bien presente
su deber a la enseñanza,
preparar a nuestra gente
sin perder esa esperanza.

La tierra se lo tragó.
La tierra se lo ha tragado.
Sus hazañas vivirán
y nunca será olvidado.

Bueno, señores letrados
todos en esta nación,
hay que seguir el ejemplo
de quien vivió esta pasión.

Tomás regresa a su tierra,
Concha misma lo llevó.
Esposa digna y valiente
ese reto nos dejó.

Crystal City está de luto
mucho tiempo durará,
pues ha perdido a su hijo
que allá en el cielo andará.

La tierra se lo tragó.
La tierra se lo ha tragado.
Sus hazañas vivirán
y nunca será olvidado.

José Villarino

Corrido
Homenaje a Tomás Rivera
(*Y no se lo tragó la tierra*)*

El pueblo está entristecido
dobla su rostro en dolor
por nuestro hermano querido
hombre recto y cumplidor.

Sus esfuerzos fueron tantos
que no se pueden contar
como nos dice Hinojosa
él los pudo soportar.

Vuela vuela palomita
anda cuéntale a la gente
Coro diles que Tomás Rivera
es un hombre muy decente.

Tomás Rivera nacido
en el pueblo de Cristal
donde nace raza noble
raza mestiza y cabal.

Con delicadez les canto
notas para contemplar
los siguientes versos cuentan
de su vida y su penar.

Vuela paloma enlutada
por favor no llores más
Coro háblanos con alegría
de nuestro amigo Tomás.

*This *corrido* was written in September 1984 by Dr. José Villarino of San Diego State University, San Diego, California. It was first performed by Fernando Tapia and José Licano Palma, both graduate students at the University of Arizona (Tucson), at the "Gran Concurso de Corridos" in the Tucson Meet Yourself festival, October 11, 1986. The annual *corridos* competition is organized by Dr. Celestino Fernández, sociologist and Associate Vice President for Academic Affairs at the University of Arizona (Tucson), and sponsored by the Southwest Folklore Center of the same institution. The *corrido* was recorded by José "Pepe" Villarino, José Licano Palma, Roberto Costales, and Adolfo "Pelón" Saucedo on December 20, 1986, at the University of Arizona. Dr. Villarino also recognizes the contributions of Oscar Galván and Dr. Arturo Ramírez of San Diego State University.

Desde chico puso ejemplo
trabajando con fervor
de Tejas a Minnesota
demostrando su valor.

Esos tiempos fueron duros
sin unión ni protección
nunca abandonó la lucha
siempre con dedicación.

Vuela vuela palomita
anda grítale a la gente
Coro   que viva Tomás Rivera
sendero resplandeciente.

Era un hombre de principios
no lo podemos dudar
las cosas que Tomás hizo
no se pueden olvidar.

Oigan hermanos chicanos
pónganme mucha atención
nunca se den por vencidos
y sigan su educación.

Vuelva paloma bronceada
anda grítale a la gente
Coro   su partida no fue en vano
y él vivirá para siempre.

Que su triunfo sea un ejemplo
pa toda la juventud
que todos sigan sus pasos
con fuerza y con rectitud.

Un consejo sólo dejo
ya casi pa terminar
que no olviden a su raza
allí está su bienestar.

Vuela paloma viajera
llévatelo en tu vuelo
Coro   anda cuéntale a la gente
que estamos todos de duelo.

Vuela paloma dorada
lleva a cada uno una rosa
Coro   una a cada de sus hijos
y una a su querida esposa.

Vuela vuela palomita
grita por toda la sierra
Coro   aquí está Tomás Rivera
no se lo tragó la tierra.

Alurista

bartolo's kuilmas

u remember, tomás?
smile, source
power, stalk
column, spinal?
   . . . no, pos sí!
u remember, tomás?
wine, grape
thought, treasure
heart, dice?
   . . . no, pos sí!
u remember, tomás?
rosarito lobster
awe, brilliance
impeccable self?
   . . . no, pos sí?
u remember, tomás?
the paper poet's dawn?
the sand dunes
the coast?
   . . . no, pos sí!
bent back sweat
shoulders, knees
calloused hands?
   . . . no, pos sí!
i remember u,
tomás rivera
¿te acuerdas
de tu flor, tu canto
de tu llanto, tu mesquite
de tu paz, de tu armadillo?
   . . . no, pos sí!
¿te acuerdas, rivera
de las cuerdas, de la lira
del bajo sexto, del acordeón
de las barras, de la chancla?
   . . . no, pos sí!
¿te acuerdas, rivera
de las olas, las veredas
de las estrellas, las rocas
de la espuma, del ocelote?

¿te acuerdas, rivera
del mar, del océano
del río, del valle
de la lucha, de la raza
   . . . no, pos sí!
¿te acuerdas, rivera
   . . . no, pos sí, cómo no?
remember, tomás?
stark smile, yes
pleased with life
no complaints
   . . . sí, pos no!
i remember tomás
telling him, even
that angry hearts throb
that "greens" treasure
   . . . sí, pos no! no bombs!
i remember tomás
he say to me "hail
   . . . believe in no führer!
b yourself, suffer not!
   . . . sí, pos no!
i remember tomás
he say "size b
a measure from the head
to the sky, lest it b
to the dust and dirt"
   . . . sí, pos no!
i remember tomás
yes
i remember your joy
tomás
me acuerdo, rivera
de tus ojos certeros
de tu palabra breve
de tu aura y obra
   . . . sí, pos no!
me decías cuando
cuestionaba yo, tanto
y con causa me rebelaba
   . . . sí, pos no!
me decías "¡lucha
no te dejes, ni apendejes
sigue tu vereda!"
me acuerdo, rivera
que tú te acordabas
que tú amabas
que tú laborabas
que tú luchabas

me acuerdo, rivera
¿me olvido . . .?
    . . . sí, pos no!
¿cómo sacarte de mi alma?
"¡sácate la daga!"
me dijiste alguna vez
contestándote yo dije
" 'ta bien,
dejemos que'l tío sam
nos dé posada . . ."
". . . sí, pos no,
mejor a maría y a josé
¡pos en este mundo
tiene uno que andar
con mula!" con sonrisa
replicaste, rivera
te pregunté entonces, tomás
que si la libertad valía,
que si la autodeterminación,
la nuestra, que si américa era
un solo continente
que si lograríamos ser
nosotros mismos
que si nuestra palabra
cruzaría el tiempo,
el espacio, las fronteras
las galaxias, que si seríamos
al fin, uno, un solo pueblo
una sola tierra
y tú dijiste
". . . sí, pos claro
. . . no, pos desde luego
. . . sí, por supuesto
no pos . . . sin lugar a dudas"
. . . claro, tomás rivera, claro
¡no, no has desaparecido!
¡sí, sí estás presente!
esta daga se queda . . .
esta espina no daña . . .
esta flor no perece . . .
este canto no calla . . .
este canto no calla . . .
. . . este canto no calla

Roberto A. Galván

**Un acróstico
A la memoria de
Tomás Rivera**

Tu Cristal no tuvo abono, ni
Olor
    a tierra mojada, y
¡Mira qué cosechaste!, y
Aun labrando en
    las *labores*
Sin raíces arraigadas

Retaste a tu manera, e
Impulsado
    en la torrente
Venciste,
    te impusiste, y
El dique de las barreras
Rodó con prejuicio
    y todo
Ante el timón de tu barca.

Paul Trujillo

A Child Was Born

For Tomás Rivera

And raised with flowers.
And the darkness of the soil
on his hands amazed him.
As he grew he learned
of the ways of gardens,
how the roots sustain,
how the vines give birth
above ground and swaying
in the open air, how
the reticent carrot will try to hide
its bright fruit in darkness.
And he learned
with sweetness
of a world beneath worlds
from which colors like flags
unfurl and wash
into the landscape of the living.
But from the gardens of his childhood
a boy had grown
who would learn, in schools,
of the painfulness of difference,
who would hide, among graveyards,
his tears of salt
that turned to glass.
In each tear a world
took shape
and crystalized. And the words
of epitaphs engraved on stone
or carved in wood
etched on his heart
the lament of love: Remember me . . . always.
But even the boy would grow
with change
though he remained a rose
and with the darkest of petals
that would fall as words.
And in the words were tears
wrung from a wound

of desires and laughter
(each scar grew eyes
that saw suffering through love).
And in the words were lives
where flesh and bone,
confused with shadows,
screamed out in anguish
as the truest of prayers—a mother
crying madly for her absent son.
Or the words became pollen
because the child took root
with understanding of the darkness,
growing silent as a dove
about to sleep, and in the highest
of all branches.
Now he is sleeping. Only sleeping.
See the angel that guards him,
how its hand extends to shade his eyes?
A child was born and raised with flowers.

Irene I. Blea

generation

you have honored us
    by moving forward
        with few others
            of your generation
you have honored us
    by being pioneers
        by breaking paths
            to foreign doors
you and the men
    of your age
        wrote the unwritten story
            in the spoken language
you have honored us
    by taking pen to paper
        thoughts from your mind
           by sharing
you have honored us
    by speaking about causes
        treaties broken
           some never spoken
you and the men
    of your generation
        honor us with
           motivation

losing

we have lost one more
    one more gifted and talented
        chicano human being
we have lost him
    from our community
        from our institutions
            from our scholarship
                from our presence
there is one less person
    to address chicano issues
        there is one less friend
            one less husband
                one less brother
                    one less son
one more body
    will not be present
        neither will one more laughter
            one more spirit
            one more prayer
we have lost one more
    gifted
        talented
            sharing
                thinking
                  talking
                    human being

Pat Mora

Tomás Rivera

They knew so much, his hands
spoke of the journey from Crystal City
to Iowa, Michigan, Minnesota, year after year
dirt-dusted in fields and orchards,
his hands a pillow at night,
in bare, cold buildings,
family laughter in his favorite blanket.

On slow days his hands
gathered books at city dumps,
saved like the memories of smiling
hard at that first grade teacher
and her noises in the other language
that didn't laugh like Spanish.

Those hands clenched in the dark
at *víboras, víboras* hissing
       we don't want you. you people have lice
as the school door slammed
but Tomás learned
and his hands began to hold books
gently, with affection. He searched
for stories about his people and finally
gave their words sound, wrote the books
he didn't have, we didn't have.

And he graduated over and over
until one day he was Chancellor Rivera
famous Chicano, too needed,
his hands too full of us
to sit alone and write green stories
alive with voices, "fiesta of the living,"
pressing, the present pressing
like the hands reaching out to him
and he'd hug the small, brown hands
his hands whispering his secret
             learn, learn
his face a wink, teasing out their smiles,
a face all could rest in,
like the cherries he picked, dark,

sweet, round a pit, tooth-breaker
for the unwary, the lazy, the cruel.

His hands knew about the harvest,
tasted the laborer's sweat in the sweet
cantaloupes he sliced, knew how to use
laughter to remove stubborn roots
of bitter weeds: prejudice, indifference,
the boy from Crystal City, Texas
not a legend to be shelved
but a man whose *abrazos* still warm
us yet say, "Now you."

María Alicia Arrizón

A don Tomás Rivera

Cómo podré expresar o definir
la huella
el rostro
todo lo que has dejado:
un mundo lleno de realidades
que nos hacen
palpar
devorar
cada momento impreso
de tu existencia.

Naciste recorriendo
el camino de la lucha:
sufriste
ganaste
para después marcharte
(diz que al más allá)
al vivir eterno.

El mañana y el ayer
siempre serán tuyos:
tuyo todo
todo lo tuyo
que quedó estampado
en la tierra
en los corazones
del peregrino
en Aztlán.

Alfonso Rodríguez

A Tomás Rivera in Memoriam

> Who has twisted us around like this, so that
> no matter what we do, we are in the posture
> of someone going away? Just as, upon
> the farthest hill, which shows him his whole valley
> one last time, he turns, stops, lingers—,
> so we live here, forever taking leave.
>
> Rainer Maria Rilke, *The eighth elegy*

    Bajó la primavera
sus defensas
        y descendió de golpe
el filo de un invierno
           hacia nosotros
De repente nada tiene sentido
      nada importa
    ni la amenaza
de un próximo holocausto
    ni las auroras lejanas
que acaso jamás disfrutaremos
    ni los sutiles momentos
que dan color a la existencia
    ni el sonido indescifrable
de cada gota de vida que bebemos
    ni los estares ni los seres
    ni los dóndes ni los cuándos
        Nada
Sólo esta herida
    mañosamente intrusa
      y un lúgubre silencio
         insoportable

¿Qué fue lo que sentiste
    en el momento en que la voluntad
      se te nublaba?
¿Qué nombre invocaste cuando te alejabas?
¿De qué verdad perdurable te agarraste?
      Pobre Tomás, dirán algunos,
  se le agotaron los resortes
Pero hermano:
      ¡qué enorme cantidad de vida

cayó sobre tus hombros!
Y tú te la bebiste apresuradamente
porque querías engendrar más vida
¿Cuánta sangre hay que entregar
para dar la misión por terminada?
       ¿Cuántas veces lo abandonamos todo
       sólo para volver a empezar
       sólo para volver a bajar los mismos escalones
       hacia el mismo inframundo
       de miradas opacas
       y palabras portadoras de tinieblas
                      buscando la esperanza?

¿Cuántas veces te dieron ganas de ser piedra?
¿O ser un tosco tronco arrojado a la orilla del camino?
¿O mejor una mancha en el cielo casi desdibujada
                      para que el viento te borrara?
       Tal vez en cierto modo
No obstante,
              a ti te impulsaba
                     el fuego de otra sangre
una sangre que fue propicia
                     a tus motivos
una sangre que se reparte
                     en el camino
Tú nos enseñaste
       a no llevar la vida encima
       como uniforme ajado

       Bendito sea Dios, Tomás,
porque tú no dudaste
              de que la Vida
                     había puesto un día
                           dos alas a tu alcance
       Una vez te refugiaste
en lo profundo de ti mismo
y luego surgiste renovado
              entre esta proliferación
                     siniestra
                            de espejismos
              entre la rémora de un tiempo
                     manipulado
                           con astucia
       Emprendiste tu vuelo
y volaste muy alto
sin alejarte de nosotros
              devorando significantes
                     y significados
              elaborando imágenes

                              y símbolos
                        que surgían
                        de la sufrida hondura
                              de tu pueblo
                        filtrándose en el caudal creativo
                              de tu mente
            con ese testimonio de varón maduro
            con esa urgencia de entregarte en cuerpo y alma
            con esa terquedad de darles forma y fundamento
                              a tantas inquietudes
                              a tantas esperanzas

                  Después
            llegó lo que ninguno sospechaba
            irrumpió el otro lado
                              en este lado
            Y tú sentiste el toque de lo eterno
                        en un momento cotidiano
            En este lado
                  la palabra es borrosa
                        casi oscura
            Y tú quisiste darle luz a tu manera

                  ¿Cómo debemos recordarte?
            No sabemos
            Cada cual acoplará
                  el recuerdo
                  a su experiencia
            Como quiera que sea
                  gracias, hermano,
                  por la porción de tiempo
                        y la porción de espacio
                        que compartiste con nosotros
            Gracias
            por todo lo que fuiste
                  y sigues siendo

                  Algún día alguien te llamará
            reparador de sueños estropeados
            y en tardes apacibles, en otra primavera,
            muchos saldrán a recoger
                  la cosecha
                        de todos los sueños
                              que has sembrado

VI.   *Essays and Lectures for Tomás Rivera*

SEARCHING:
WHEN OLD DREAMS FIND THEIR YOUTH AGAIN

*John David Maguire**

The poem is called "The Searchers" (see Section II of this volume). This first Tomás Rivera lecture—more meditation than lecture—is intensely personal, for it reflects upon six elements that were at the center of a friend's incandescent life, cut short. He shared with us the passion of *his* prophecy. The question is whether we can make good its promises. This talk is a call for us to render real in the public world those commitments that constituted this good man's life and were his search.

I

The first element is compassion: *com-passione*, the capacity to "suffer with." Tomás was possessed of that. Following a meeting to plan a conference, when I had decried the encroaching tyranny, as well as the frequent aridity, of statistics, charts, and graphs, I jokingly challenged him to produce some figures that stirred the blood. I was unprepared for what I received two days later—a neatly typed half page with no heading, that simply began:

—Almost 1,300,000 Texas women live below the poverty line: This figure represents 16 percent of all Texas women, or more than one in six.

—Almost 1,000,000 Texas children live in poverty, or almost one in five.

—More than 158,000 female-headed Texas families live below the poverty line: Almost 52,500 are Mexican-American.

—Texas now has 90,000 indigent pregnant women, and, of that number, 50,000 are receiving incomplete prenatal care or none at all—the absence of which increases a baby's chances of dying by 40 percent.

—The Census Bureau announced in January 1984 that the number of Americans living below the poverty line had increased by over 9,000,000—or 35 percent—in the four years between 1979 and 1983. The proportion of Americans living in poverty is now higher than at any time since before the War on Poverty began in 1965. The total number of poor people in the United States in March 1984 was 35,300,000.

—More than one in seven Americans is poor today, compared to one in nine in 1979. More than 13.3 million children are poor—3.3 million more than in 1979.

—Almost half of all Black children are poor, and over half the Black female-headed families are poor.

*This paper was presented as a distinguished lecture in memory of Tomás Rivera at the 1985 National Conference on Higher Education of the American Association for Higher Education. The Tomás Rivera Lecture has been given yearly since his death.

Looking at that piece of paper Tomás had sent, I suddenly recalled Dos Passos's remark: "Our only hope will lie in the frail web of understanding of one person for the pain of another." And I realized, sharply and with some shame, how I, we, turn away from the statistics of misery, the facts of pain, the figures reflecting anguish and suffering. It is too easy to forget the other America, to insulate ourselves, to refuse to see, or, worse yet, try to redefine into acceptability, searing, crushing, killing poverty.

Any reflection on Tomás has to begin here, with this quality that underlies all the others: compassion. Fidelity to his legacy—which is what I am urging—surely requires that we seek to cultivate this quality in *our* lives.

II

Move swiftly to a second element, the realities of status and power, to which he gave considerable attention. Tomás knew of the bonds between the powerful and the powerless—that it needn't be the case but is too often, that power is achieved at the expense of the powerless.

I shared with him some remarks of Bernie Harleston, the president of City College of the City University of New York, and he agreed that we should make something like them the text for the conference we were planning and had rather blandly titled "Education Coherence in a Multi-Cultural Society." Harleston wrote:

> Opportunity is being replaced as a term in the public debate on access to education by "academic excellence." The claim of a growing chorus is that we need to demand more of our students, we need to improve their performance on standardized tests, we need to revamp the educational system so that we produce a population of high achievers. But the undercurrent in the debate is that we need to limit access to educational institutions. When all the euphemisms are eliminated and the jargon peeled away, the core of the argument advanced by the critics is that access should be limited to those students who are destined to be successes in the academic world.
>
> But what of those who by virtue of the circumstances of their birth or their early exposure, the color of their skin or their Spanish surname are destined, *without access to education*, to be excluded from the job market, the housing market, the marketplace of life? Should not all who want a higher education have that opportunity, not just those whom circumstances permitted to go to the best primary and secondary schools under the best of circumstances?
>
> Look at the facts and begin at the beginning. What does it mean that 40 to 50 percent of the kids in our urban high schools drop out, and what of the even higher cumulative dropout rate of minority teenagers? We must talk first about and act first on the issue of how we keep these young people in school. *Then* we can talk and act on how we upgrade and insure the quality of their educational experiences. This is the reality of the present crisis in America's education. If we do not confront directly, openly, and with compassion the realities of the dropout phenomenon, our collective concern about "quality" will amount to a functional hill of beans—and will lack integrity and moral persuasion.
>
> It is healthy, and important, for this country to get excited about education. But, we have to be careful that we do not allow education to become the target, and the only target, at which we aim our anxieties about immigration, about social welfare programs, about federalism, about international capitalism, and about the development of our national strength.

I heard echoes in Harleston's analysis of the scathing critique of the times by the 19th century feminist critic and activist Fanny Wright:

> Do not the rich command instruction, and they who have instruction, must they not possess the power? And when they have the power, will they not exert it in their own favour? While the many are left in ignorance, the few—though powerful—cannot be wise for, having not shared, they cannot be virtuous.

Tomás believed passionately in education: *e-ducere,* leading people out. He believed that education represented a route to power that was not achieved at others' expense, education as a non-"zero-sum" approach to power. He *knew* that in knowledge lies power and that people denied access to knowledge are doomed to discouragement and despair, to apathy or anger, to bitterness and self-hate. Provided access and support, the sky's their limit. His life and those of his students proved it. Not everyone will reach the top, as the world judges it. He knew that. Indeed, he once reminded a group of progress-preoccupied business leaders probing the virtues of the humanities: "I believe in the indispensability of the humanities because, through them, one studies failure as well as success. The humanities depict 'firsts' but they also portray and illumine 'seconds,' 'thirds,' and 'fourths.'"

When I asked him about that he replied, "People have got to be freed even to be 'fourths.' Otherwise they might be 'tenths' and feel like 'zeroes.' They've got to get out of places with iron bars at the windows and iron gates at the door."

Tomás linked power with education. Education was the surest route to permanent empowerment, he believed. It was education that provided the means by which people moved their lives from bondage—to ignorance, superstition, deprivation—toward freedom—the chance to decide some things for oneself, to have some walkin'-around room.

That is what denying education to people was, for him, immoral and criminal, for by that action, he reasoned, those denied are deprived of the chance for movement, for participation, for so many of life's pleasures, for freedom.

"Unshackle them" was one of his watchwords. In this interweaving of education and knowledge with status and power, Tomás believed with Emily Dickinson:

> We never know how high we are
> 'Til we are asked to rise
> And then if we are true to plan
> Our statures touch the skies.

III

Tomás knew the indissoluble connections between the body and the body politic, which leads us directly to the central element or passion of his public life: the preoccupation with justice. At that same business leaders' meeting he declared, "There is a sense in which all reading, all study, but particularly reading in the humanities, puts one in touch with the oldest human value—justice." He loved and quoted John Rawls' statement: "Justice is the first virtue of social institutions." *Jus-titia*: literally the fulfillment of reason's (i.e., reasonable) expectations. It means weighing well and acting appropriately. Justice humanizes power, making power not an end in itself, but a means of redeeming the powerless. In our time, justice means fairness, integrity, but preeminently empowerment and equity, equitable empowerment.

He deplored what he called the indisputable facts of injustice in American higher education, pointing to the time just a few years ago when no Chicanos occupied positions of power in the entire American university world, then the phase of the "onlys"—as he was the only chancellor-level Chicano administrator in the entire United States—and the way the "firsts" too often remain the "onlys." He decried the way in which Blacks, Hispanics, and Native Americans composed a disproportionately high percentage of those made victim by the cuts in financial aid for college-age, qualified, but needy, potential students, the way in which the reduction in such aid is reflected across the country in a major decline in the number of minority students enrolling in four-year, post-baccalaureate institutions, the way in which low-income and minority students are receiving a declining proportion of student financial assistance.

Today, enrollment of undergraduate minority students is down at most institutions across the country and at virtually all the prestige institutions, a fact that extends to the professional schools and to the graduate schools of these institutions. He decried the indisputable fact that there has been a decline in active recruiting of minorities; there has been a reduction in the percent of budget allocated to financial aid; there has been an increase—a very significant increase—in the proportion of the financial aid budgets of our institutions allocated to enrolling competitive, non-needy students. He knew that this abdication of a commitment to meet real financial need insures that fewer minority students will be able to enroll in colleges and universities across this country. That, he knew, was an injustice.

He believed that so-called social progress had been unjustly arrested in the last few years and that the nation was shamelessly backsliding into the inequity he had struggled all his life to overcome.

He grew increasingly impatient with the argument, already noted, that a "recovery of quality" in education—which he, a person of impeccable intellectual standards, was all for—somehow meant turning away the initially underprepared or offering students only an Anglo-European course of studies. He was increasingly concerned that the growing invocation of quality was leading operationally to the denial of equity. For him, "quality" achieved at the price of opportunity and equity was not quality. He would have agreed fully with Irving Spitzberg:

> It is imperative that every discussion of quality acknowledge and reject any cost in terms of opportunity and that standards be constrained by an equally strong commitment to equity. It will not be good enough to invoke quality if we forget equity. Nor will we create equality of opportunity if our strategies for equity are at the expense of the quality of the opportunity. We will achieve neither equity nor quality if we do not give careful attention to our policy goals and to the strategies for implementing change consistent with these goals.

Tomás's passion for justice was not limited to the struggle for equitable education. He deplored injustice everywhere and that burning indignation cost him years off his life. When people hurt and are in pain and are brutalized, it got to him. In a world where Mexican kids die in ditches trying to get across, where people seeking a sanctuary have to shiver with fear in rat-filled basements, where the jobless are hungry and homeless, where people sleep in gutters, where the poor ache and despair, where a kid gets beaten up because he can't say what he feels in English, there, he believed, is injustice and *we* have to do something about it. We are morally lost, he believed, if we turn away, retreat, let that capacity for indignation wane. If we try to flee politics, rush headlong into private life and shut the door, then we're dead before we die. It is not difficult to issue *pronunciamientos* denouncing injustice. The hard task is to figure our how to render one's commitment to justice operational. What will really work? What practically should we do to assure that empowerment is done more equitably? How can we reverse unjust policies, put an end to inequitable practices? War is won in the trenches, not back at staff headquarters. Practical, field-centered programs were what we should be turning our imaginations toward. Most of all, he believed that any lasting progress is achieved through coalitions, not by any group's attempting to go it alone.

The destiny of searchers, Tomás averred, is to seek justice for *everybody* in *every dimension* of human existence. He cheered W. H. Auden's call:

Clear away from your heads the masses of impressive rubbish.
Rally the lost and trembling forces of the will.
Gather them up and let them loose upon the Earth
'Til they construct at last a human justice.

IV

Heavy? Heavy indeed. For with that indignation there also is fear. In Tomás, however, the indignation was kept from turning to bitterness by a persistent power of wonder and a capacity for playfulness. Professor Albert Rabil recently wrote:

> Wonder is the way we open ourselves and stay open rather than closing ourselves and getting cut off. Human growth—individually or institutionally—comes by incorporating or integrating new material into our old ways, our old selves, so that the whole situation becomes changed. The capacity that is required for this growth is wonder, the ability to be open, to be like those children who can be stupendously in awe at everything about them.
>
> Wonder is limited by fear. Wherever fear is, there is the boundary-marker—for learning, for growth, for maturing. And the thing we seem to fear most—wherever the fear comes from—is *failure*. We create 'a world' in which we are relatively safe, in which we know how to function. When something 'new' penetrates that world (and the older we become it is change of any sort or being forced to concede that our verities may be neither absolute nor eternal), it is threatened with coming unglued, we are faced with the uncertain, we do not know whether we can handle it, and we become nervous, seeking either to expel the intruder or incorporate it in a 'safe' way into our functioning universe. But what if we could respond not out of fear but out of wonder? Where there's no wonder or where wonder ceases and fear begins, we will find, in every case, our personal boundaries or limits. A sure sign of wonder is the manifested capacity for play.

A joke at just the right moment, often corny but on target, a reminder not to take it all too seriously, most of all ourselves. Tomás had that.

He knew fear, never doubt that. His world was as distracting as ours: beset by deadening noise, swamped by hype, intruded upon by gossip, beset by doubts and worries. But he was kept from paralysis by wonder, that boyish, playful openness, and by an imagination that never became fettered. Openness to the new, the novel, the exploding image—sometimes sweat-soaked, blood-spattered, other times ecstasy-uttering, love-sounding. Tomás was open to, he sought to shape, the illuming image. "Never underestimate the power of the image," he once counseled. Images carry dreams, they embody visions, they permit the body to focus on something important—a goal, a challenge, an as-yet unrealized future. Oh, the power of images, products of a playful imagination.

Tomás looked at the world with a roaming eye and a sense of the possibility of something still new. The world to Tomás, full of suffering, to be sure, remained wonder-full. He was redeemed from the melancholic by the power of his wonder-filled imagination.

V

There is another theme as central to Tomás's vision as his passion for justice: his conviction that we are all connected. He once commented on the Polish Peoples' movement. "That's a great name for a movement, *Solidarity*." He would—indeed, in his own words and language, he did—echo Martin Luther King, Jr.: "If any are enslaved, we are not free. If any are sick, none of us is completely well; as long as there's war in the world, none of us is completely at peace." Hunger must be overcome. Poverty ameliorated. Peace achieved.

Freedom realized. At that meeting on the humanities with business leaders I quoted Andrew Young:

> If we help others, all will be well; if we do not, nothing matters. The rich cannot prosper without progress by the poor. It will not be possible for any nation or group of nations to save itself either by dominion *over* others or by isolation from them. On the contrary, real progress will be made nationally only if it can be assured globally.

No sooner had I finished than Tomás sent me a note that read simply: "Amen! Amen!"

Tomás believed that we are all connected. To paraphrase the old children's hymn, "Red, yellow, black, and white. All are precious to the sight". . . . of those who have the eyes of prophecy. This dimension of Tomás's commitment often slips by under the rubric "internationalism." It was that, to be sure, and no wonder that he championed cross-cultural studies. But his was a vivid, palpable internationalism, the sense that my destiny is linked to that of a Scandinavian housewife or a Japanese fisherman, and that I am somehow diminished if they are. If they—the "theys" anywhere in the world—are in bondage, so, to some extent, am I.

Not so long ago, I encountered a most arresting essay by a young Los Angeles writer, Michael Ventura, that concludes with a longish passage that perfectly reflects Tomás's sense that we are all connected, indeed, that captures the conviction with a metaphor at the heart of Tomás's reality, *marriage.* We're all *wed, married*, to each other:

Ventura writes:

> The dream we must now seek to realize, the new human project, is not "*security*" which is impossible to achieve on the planet Earth in the latter half of the 20th century. It is not "*happiness*," by which we generally mean nothing but giddy forgetfulness about the dangers of all our lives together. It is not "*self-realization*," by which people usually mean a separate peace. There is no separate peace. "While there is a soul in prison, I am not free," said Eugene Debs once upon a time, and that goes for all sorts of prisons, psychic as well as walled. The real project is to realize that technology has married us all to each other, has made us one people on one planet and that until we are more courageous about this new marriage—our selves all intertwined—there will be no peace and the destination of any of us will be unknown.
>
> This project requires a new understanding that we are many selves, not just one self, as well as a new approach to our institutions—a reordering of them in more decentralized, inclusive, human ways.
>
> How far can we go together . . . men and women, black, brown, yellow, white, young and old? We will go as far as we can because we must go wherever it is we are going together. There is no such thing as going alone. Given the dreams and doings of our psyches, given the nature of our world, there is no such thing as *being* alone. If you are the only one in the room it is still a crowded room.
>
> But we are all together on this planet Earth, you, me, us; inner, outer, together and we're called to affirm our marriage vows. Our project, the new human task, is to learn how to consummate, how to sustain, how to enjoy this most human marriage—all parts, all of us.

VI

Steadfastness suffused by hope. Toward the end of one of those sometimes discouraging initial sessions for planning the policy analysis center that now bears his name, when several of us had questioned its feasibility—whether we could get the support such a venture required—Tomás casually remarked, "I'd rather live with my hope than their doubts." That is the comment of a person who remains true to his vision throughout, despite his clear-headed awareness that his vision finds only fitful realization in American life today, and that the situation of those he cared most about might be worsening. He was concerned about the growing national mood of mean-spiritedness and cavalier disregard for whole groups, be they bankrupt farmers or indentured students. And yet he persisted in that broad and generous vision of how all humankind might live together, risking more in the name of full human connection, acknowledging that we are not alone if only we will share our touch, our feeling, which is, after all, all that we have.

For too many human beings, he knew, things are terrible. But with hope, the picture is not wholly bleak; with steadfast courage, the fight is still not wholly over.

Pick up any strand of his life, any piece of his prose, any fragment of his poems, or a short story, or any one of those policy statements he had time to write out and you will find that those elements *were* his life: compassion, the sense of the relation between education and knowledge and power and status, his passion for justice, his sense of wonder and capacity for playfulness, his conviction that we're all interconnected, and his commitment to persevering, with hope—to keeping alive the human imagination. We are not alone. We are not alone in death.

With the substitution of Tomás Rivera's name for Paul Klee's in Howard Nemerov's luminous poem, "The Painter Dreaming in the Scholar's House," I close with this reflection upon our poet-educator-friend:

> These thoughts have chiefly been about [Tomás Rivera],
> About how he in our hard time might stand to us
> Especially whose lives concern themselves with learning
> As patron of the practical intelligence of art,
> and thence as model, modest and humorous in sufferings,
> For all research that follows spirit where it goes.
> That there should be much goodness in the world,
> Much kindness and intelligence, candor and charm,
> And that it all goes down in the dust after a while,
> This is a subject for the steadfast meditations
> Of the heart and mind, as for the tears
> That clarify the eye toward charity.
> So may it be to all of us, that at some times
> In this bad time when faith in study seems to fail,
> And when impatience in the street and still despair at home
> Divide the mind to rule it, there shall some comfort come
> From the remembrance of so deep and clear a life as his
> Whom I have thought of, for the wholeness of his mind,
> As the painter dreaming in the scholar's house,
> His dream an emblem to us of the life of thought.

Those of us whose lives will always be touched by Tomás's owe it to him to live our lives with his singularity of purpose and, as nearly as we can manage, with his courage and integrity, sensitive to human need, passionate for social justice, committed to "taming the heart of mankind and making gentle the life of the world."

Tomás was an old vision for whose realization *we* still must seek, an old dream searching to become young again. Tomás Rivera was our sorrow for mankind's inhumanity. He is our pledge to make it whole.

CLAREMONT UNIVERSITY

FACING THE FACTS ABOUT MEXICAN AMERICA

Alfredo G. de los Santos, Jr.

> when we walked
> all over Minnesota
> looking for work
> No one seemed to care
> we did not expect them to care

These five lines are from one of Tomás Rivera's poems, "The Searchers." As I present my sense of reality in Mexican America,[1] please keep them in mind.

> when we walked
> all over Minnesota
> looking for work
> No one seemed to care
> we did not expect them to care

I feel uneasy—and somewhat uncomfortable—being in a city where policy is set that mortgages the future of countless generations for *destruction*, instead of for *construction*, development and nurturing.

I feel uneasy—and somewhat uncomfortable—being in a city where the highest education officer of the land, to quote Matthew Prophet, superintendent of schools in Portland, Oregon, sacrifices "public education on the altar of political expediency."

I feel uneasy—and somewhat uncomfortable—being in a city where the only number that is increasing faster every year than the national debt and the defense budget is the percent of children who live in poverty in this country.

It is a delight and an great honor for me to be invited to present this, the second Tomás Rivera Lecture, co-sponsored by the American Association for Higher Education and the AAHE Hispanic Caucus.

It is fitting that at this *national* conference on higher education we should be addressing a *regional* reality, because what takes place in Mexican America has significant implications not only regionally, but also nationally and internationally. It is clear to me that most things in life are interrelated and interdependent. Countries are interrelated and dependent on each other; the same is true of generations of people. And it is also true of the institution that we call education. All its component parts are interrelated and interdependent.

Interdependency

Unlike those whom Tomás Rivera saw as uncaring, we must all care because more and more we depend on one another. Countries are interdependent. The Spring 1985 issue of *The Borderlands Journal* describes the United States-Mexico border as "a unique ambience of human interdependence—culturally, socially, and economically." That special issue ad-

---

*The 1986 Tomás Rivera Lecture was presented at the National Conference on Higher Education of the American Association for Higher Education, Washington, D.C., March 13, 1986.

dresses the ways in which the customs, values, mores, and ethics of each country are influenced by the other.[2] Border towns still remember "Black Thursday," the day in 1982, when the Mexican peso plunged and retail stores on both sides of the border went out of business and unemployment soared.[3] This interdependence affects both Mexicans and Americans; in the Texas border communities of McAllen, Brownsville, Laredo, and El Paso, 30 percent of the Hispanic families are below the poverty level.[4] The plunge of the peso had—and continues to have—international repercussions. Thus, the interdependency of countries is direct and immediate.

The interdependence among generations does not seem as direct and immediate, but it is there. Generally speaking, the young in most societies are nurtured, cared for, and educated by the adults. In our society, we also make provision for the older, retired adults through such institutions and programs as Medicare, Medicaid, and Social Security. The quality and quantity of the services provided by the society to both the younger and the older generations depends on the resources that the working adults contribute in the form of taxes that sustain these institutions and programs.

All parts of the educational system are also interrelated. We in higher education are part of a single system through which people move.[5] We cannot look at higher education without acknowledging the role of the elementary and secondary level.[6] Because we are so interdependent, we must care. How Hispanic youngsters do in school is important to the future of higher education but also to the future retirees—to the future of American society.

I will paint for you a mosaic of interrelated views of reality in Mexican America. I plan to cover 1) how Chicanos are doing in higher education, 2) the role played by testing and assessment for Mexican American students, and 3) perhaps most important, what is happening to our children. With these three, I will be ready to suggest strokes which can change the picture 20-25 years from now.

Mexican America and Higher Education

While I am assuredly interested in all aspects of higher education, I am going to concentrate on community colleges, for these institutions have both benefits and liabilities to offer Mexican America. It is not new for Chicanos and other scholars to question the role of community colleges in educating Mexican Americans, as well as other minorities.[7] Community colleges are said to perpetuate the present social and economic inequities because of tracking systems which keep minorities segregated, because of vocational curricula which prepare minorities for low skill jobs, because of high minority drop out rates, and because of the few minority students who transfer to universities and earn baccalaureate degrees.[8]

However, it is probably not fruitful to criticize community colleges because they have not been able to right all the wrongs associated with social inequality and economic discrimination.[9] For one thing, community colleges are unique and the students they serve are special. Their student population includes those with less academic preparation than most university students. Most of the students are part-time, commute to school, and can afford only the less expensive community colleges. Most are females. Most work and of those who work most do so on a full-time basis. Perhaps the best way to describe community college students is to use the term "swirling." They swirl from the community college to the university, to work, back to the community college, back to work, and on and on.[10]

Despite the weaknesses, community colleges are important to Mexican Americans. Community colleges provide their major initial—and for a lot, the only—access to higher education. On a national level, about 60 percent of all Hispanics enrolled in higher education are in two-year institutions.[11] In California, 85 percent are enrolled in two-year colleges.[12] Because Hispanics, as a group, are without funds needed to attend four-year institutions, the community college will continue to be the primary access for Hispanics to higher education. [13]

There is still much work to be done. Mexican-American students need better instruction. While all minority groups improved SAT scores in 1985, Mexican Americans had average verbal and math scores 50 points below the average of all students. [14]

Mexican-American students need to be encouraged to stay in school. While Hispanic high school graduates increased 38 percent from 1975 to 1982, Hispanic enrollment in college decreased 16 percent. [15] There are several reasons for this decline. First, educational costs, even at a community college, are now higher. Second, the change in financial aid from grants to loans has led to a perception, if not a reality, that financial aid is not available. Third, a lot of young people are attracted to the armed forces. Fourth, admissions standards of institutions have increased. The final reason for a decline among Hispanics enrolled in college is the increased use of assessment.

This leads me directly to my next point—the place of testing and assessment in the education of Mexican Americans.

Testing/Assessment and Mexican America

Chicano leaders have criticized standardized tests because they represent a White middle-class bias of both culture and language which puts Mexican American students at a disadvantage. In addition to the *tests themselves*, we must address the problem of *misuse of tests*. I am concerned about the impact on Mexican America of three different misuses of tests in education: 1) heavy reliance on testing for admissions, 2) testing to predict college success, and 3) teacher testing.

The Mexican-American Legal Defense and Educational Fund recently petitioned the presidents of the three major testing organizations that are responsible for the development and administration of standardized tests. While these organizations criticize the excessive reliance being placed on standardized tests by colleges and universities, major problems continue. There has been a rise in the use of cut-off scores for admission purposes, even though the College Board, Educational Testing Service, and American College Testing explicitly caution against such practices in their guidelines. The SAT is being used in a fashion for which it was never intended, to predict first-year performance in college. Tests are increasingly being used to solve all education's problems. Teacher testing, for example, ignores the inability to test whether a teacher has the human skills necessary for teaching. [16]

The misuse of tests that most disturbs me is teacher testing. There are three levels at which teacher testing presently occurs: *entry level* (testing which allows access to colleges of education), *certification level* (testing which certifies entry into the teaching profession), and *inservice level* (testing for those already in service to determine their continued suitability as teachers).

It is important to know that in 1985 in California, only 39 percent of Hispanic test-takers of those planning to go into teaching passed the state-required California Basic Education Skills Test, whereas 76 percent of Whites passed. [17] Some will argue that the percentage of Hispanics who pass the test is increasing. It is also true that the number of Hispanics who take the test is decreasing. That fewer Hispanics are attempting to enter the teaching profession is significant.

The most flagrant misuse of teacher testing is at the inservice level. In 1983, Greg Anrig, President of ETS, voiced his concern to the Chief State School Officers on the use of inservice testing. He said:

> Once employed, direct classroom supervision and evaluation of the teachers are possible and
> you can then assess those essential qualities of teaching competence, in addition to academic
> knowledge, that cannot be measured effectively by any paper-and-pencil evaluation—qualities
> such as dedication, sensitivity, perseverance, caring.[18]

Anrig went on to say, "The practice of requiring teachers to pass tests as a sole and determining condition of employment after they are on the job can be found in no other profession."[19]

Two years later, in 1985, Anrig reported that Texas was one of the states that had passed legislation which stipulated that "all practicing teachers—regardless of years of service and satisfactory ratings by their school supervisors—would have to pass a one-time 'functional academic skills' or 'literacy, test in order to retain their teaching certification.'"[20]

To me, the sole use of a test to make decisions about teachers who are working does not make sense. Education Testing Service has concluded that unless there is a major change in teacher preparation, minorities in the teaching force will be cut from the present 12 percent to about 6 percent.[21]

In addition to this projected 50 percent reduction of the present number of Hispanic teachers now in service, the net result of the increased use (and misuse) of testing is a sharp decline in the enrollment of Hispanics in institutions of higher education and a reduction of Hispanics seeking to become teachers.

Tomás Arciniega finds it very ironic that the standardized test, originally "conceived as a mechanism to increase access for talented youngsters of modest and poor economic circumstances . . . conceived specifically with the intent of making universities less elitist . . . these days is often viewed as serving the exact opposite function—as reducing the accessibility [of universities] . . . to Blacks, Hispanics, and other minorities most of whom come from modest and poor economic backgrounds."[22]

But to me testing is not THE problem. Testing, in my view, is a symptom, a finger pointing to the problem. Sometimes I think that we in education—when someone points a finger at a problem—spend a lot of time and energy criticizing and investigating the finger instead of dealing with the problem, in this instance the quality, or lack of it, in the education that our children are receiving. Standardized tests help us document how badly the educational system works for our children.

I am not saying that there is no problem with tests and their use and misuse. What I am saying is that tests are the finger, not the problem. And what we do now will make a significant difference in the future. For, as our children depend on us now, so will we depend on them 20-30 years hence.

Educational Prospects for Mexican-American Children

Let us examine another aspect of the mosaic—the interdependence of generations in the makeup of the population in Mexican America. Generally speaking, the Hispanic community is between 10-12 years younger than the majority. In 1984, 44 percent of Hispanics were 19 years of age or younger, compared to 28 percent for whites; 12 percent of the Hispanics were less than five years old, compared to 6 percent for whites.[23]

The average age of the white community is now about 32 or 34 years. The so-called baby boomers—now at the apex of their productivity at average ages of 35-45 years—will be thinking of retirement in some 25-30 years, around 2010.

By the year 2010, a significant percentage of the majority white community, by then retired, will be to a large degree dependent on the institutions and programs that will then be supported by the present Hispanic children.

These children are now dependent on the majority white community—the baby boomers in a lot of instances—for the education they need to be able to work so they can pay the taxes to support the institutions and programs which help sustain the whites.

Consider again how generations are interdependent. "The Dependency Ratio" is a term used to define the number of workers needed to support one retired Social Security beneficiary. In 1900, 100 workers supported less than 10 retired persons. By 1975, the ratio was 10 to 3. Several 1979 estimates suggested that by 2025, the ratio would be 2 to 1.[24] In 1981, the projected 2 to 1 ratio was moved back 20 years to 2005.[25]

By then, the retired group will become more white, while the work force becomes more varied.[26] By 2000, 1 in 3 workers will be non-white.[27] By 2000, there will be 27 million Hispanics in the United States,[28] and with the high birth rate among new immigrants, the projection could be higher.[29] So, in 2010, we can expect that in Mexican America one of the two workers supporting each retired person, most of whom will be white, will be Hispanic.

However, the educational prospects of Mexican-American children are not encouraging. Hispanics are poorer than the general population. Listen to these figures, if you will. For the last 10 years, the median family income of Hispanics has consistently been substantially below the rest of the population.[30] Some estimate that today up to 50 percent of Mexican Americans live below the poverty level.[31]

Hispanic children are about 2 1/2 times as likely as non-Hispanic white children to be poor. In 1984, about 40 percent of all Hispanic children lived in homes where the income was below the poverty level, compared to about 13 percent of non-Hispanic white children.[32] Consider that an estimated 14 million children in this country live below the poverty level and that 40 percent of the poverty population is less than 17 years old.[33] While Hispanics, who compose 20 percent of the population of Texas, have the lowest median income of any state, non-Hispanic white Texans enjoy one of the highest median income levels.[34]

The educational level of Mexican Americans is considerably below non-Hispanic whites. Among the parents of today's teenagers there is a tremendous gap in higher education experience. In Arizona, California, Colorado, New Mexico and Texas, 20-26 percent of non-Hispanic white parents have completed four or more years of college compared to 5-7 percent for Hispanic parents.[35] Among 18-24 year old Hispanics, 32-49 percent have not completed high school.[36] Yet, despite the low frequency of higher education among Mexican Americans, the education of these children is critical.

The Future of All America

The reality of Mexican America raises a basic question about the future of our country. Are we headed for a bimodal society with one group educated, white, affluent, older, and retired and the other group uneducated, minority, poor, and young? Both groups have the potential of taking more from the society than they will contribute. Perhaps, this is already beginning to happen and I don't think we can afford it.

I agree with Jerome Bruner who in 1983 wrote:

> In some way, our life as a nation depends both on cultivating intelligence to keep our complex social order running, and preventing the formation of a permanently alienated, undereducated, unemployed "under class."[37]

I submit to you that the political, economic, cultural, and social fabric of the United States cannot sustain such a future. Sometimes, in my darkest moments, when I am tired and disappointed, I wonder—deep inside—if we might become another South Africa. I think that we must decide if we want our country and our people to face a similar reality.

The business community is beginning to realize that education is part of the solution. A study funded by the California Roundtable, an organization of 90 leading corporations that study current issues of broad policy as they impact California, was recently published by Rand. They reported some fascinating data on Mexican immigration to California that lead to these findings. One, presently Mexican immigrants in California are an economic asset to the state in that their contribution to public revenue exceeds their cost of services. Two, Mexican immigrants are following historical patterns of integration into U.S. society in which successive generations move up the occupation ladder. Three, between now and 1995, 70 percent of the new jobs in California will be white collar and skilled service, and there will not be sufficient new unskilled jobs that could be expected to accommodate the projected permanent Mexican immigrants.[38] The study concluded:

> Thus, while the integration process is working well now, the changing occupational structure of the state may impede its functioning in the future. One way to avoid this potential problem is to accelerate the educational advancement of future native-born Latinos so that they will be able to qualify for jobs in the state's white collar sector, where the growth in the economy is going to occur.[39]

Policies Necessary for a Vigorous Future

The emphasis, ladies and gentlemen, has been on the wrong syllable. We have not been allocating enough resources to the greatest of our treasures—our children. We have the resources and the know-how to make the changes. We have only to decide to do it. As Frank Newman put it:

> National policy is not a result of some vast impersonal forces beyond our control. It is the sum of conscious decisions by policy makers, by institutional leaders, and by students. It is a matter of will. Both in terms of the formation of national policy and the education of the individual, what is needed is the belief that one can make a difference.[40]

It is a matter of will, but it goes beyond that. How one defines the problem influences the options for solutions. Ray Padilla put it well when he wrote to me, "Our children are not a problem. They are the solution! In any event, they are our future."[41] I have some suggestions for educational policies that will affect, not only Mexican America, but all of America.

1. Continue to insist that the educational system provide access for Mexican Americans to social and economic mobility.

2. Continue to scrutinize education preparations so that our children will do better on standardized tests, but demand that testing and assessing policies (including the correct use of tests) recognize their limitations.

3. Pay particular attention to the need for more teachers from Mexican America and other minority communities, and structure policies to ensure minority teachers will be both prepared and available.

4. Ray Padilla and Miguel Montiel suggest that in addition to participating fully in the larger political, social, cultural, economical, and educational institutions of society, we develop an educational ethic where Mexican-American education is a moral imperative.[42]

To conclude, ladies and gentlemen, I submit that the future is here! The future is now! In Mexican America, the future—here and now—is Brown . . . and progressively so. What happens in Mexican America affects us regionally, nationally, and internationally. If we do not do something—immediately—the future is bleak. No one will win; everyone will lose. If we move today to provide quality educational opportunities for *all* students, the future is bright. Everyone will win; no one will lose.

> when we walked
> all over Minnesota
> looking for work
> No one seemed to care
> we did not expect them to care

I hope that a future Chicano poet, now three to four years old or about to be born—another Tomás Rivera—will not be a member of a family that has to walk all over looking for work and will not have to write those two lines that continue to haunt me:

> No one seemed to care
> we did not expect them to care

MARICOPA COUNTY, ARIZONA,
COMMUNITY SCHOOL DISTRICT

Notes

I want to thank a large number of friends and colleagues who provided me information, ideas, articles, advice, encouragement and counsel as I worked to prepare this lecture: Greg Anrig, Carlos Arce, Tomás Arciniega, Jaime Chahin, Russ Edgerton, Rolando Hinojosa-Smith, Harold "Bud" Hodgkinson, Mari-Luci Jaramillo, Jerry R. Ladman, Arturo Madrid, John D. Maguire, Ray Padilla, and Ron Vera. I owe a special *muchas gracias* to Julie Wambach, speech faculty member at Scottsdale Community College, Arizona.

[1] *Mexican America* is the term coined by the Tomás Rivera Center to refer to the southwestern part of the United States—the states of Arizona, California, Colorado, New Mexico, and Texas.

[2] *The Borderlands Journal*, 8:2, Spring, 1985.

[3] J.R. Ladman, "The U.S. Border Regional Economy: Interdependence, Growth and Prospects for Change," in *Views Across the Border*, 2d ed., ed. S. R. Ross. Albuquerque: University of New Mexico Press, in press; "On El Main Street, U,S.A., The Birth of a New Nation," *U.S. News and World Report*, August 19, 1985, p. 33.

[4] A. Madrid, L. Estrada, R. Santos, and M. Tienda, *The Changing Profile of Mexican America: A Sourcebook for Policy Making*. Claremont, CA: Tomás Rivera Center, 1985, p. 41.

[5] H. L. Hodgkinson, *All One System: Demographics of Education, Kindergarten Through Graduate School*. Washington, D.C : Institute of Educational Leadership, 1985, p. 1.

[6] A. W. Astin, *Minorities in American Higher Education*. San Francisco: Jossey-Bass, 1982.

[7] H. Casso and G. D. Roman, eds., *Chicanos in Higher Education: Proceedings of a National Institute on Access to Higher Education for the Mexican American*. Albuquerque: University of New Mexico Press, 1976.

[8] J. Karabel, "Community Colleges and Social Stratification," *Harvard Educational Review,* 42:4:521-562, November, 1972; M. A. Olivas, *The Dilemma of Access: Minorities in Two Year Colleges*. Washington, D.C.: Howard University Press, 1979; Astin, pp. 191-192.

[9] A. M. Cohen and F. B. Brawer, *The American Community College*. San Francisco: Jossey-Bass, 1982, pp. 342-365.

[10] Ibid., p. 349.

[11] Olivas, p. 25.

[12] A. G. de los Santos, Jr., J. Montemayor, and E. Solis, Jr., "Chicano Students in Institutions of Higher Education: Access, Attrition, and Achievement," *Aztlán: International Journal of Chicano Studies Research* 14:1:96, Spring, 1983.

[13] A. G. de los Santos, Jr., "The Role of the Community College in Developing Hispanic Leadership," in *Hispanics in Higher Education: Leadership and Vision for the Next 25 Years,* ed. L. A. Valverde and S. B. García. Austin: Office for Advanced Research in Hispanic Education, University of Texas, 1982.

[14] "College Board Data Show Class of '85 Doing Better on SAT, Other Measures of Educational Attainment." New York: College Board, News release, September 23, 1985.

[15] Hodgkinson, p. 16.

[16] Letter from Ron Vera, February 13, 1986.

[17]G. R. Anrig, "Teacher Education and Teacher Testing: The Rush to Mandate." Speech presented to American Association of Colleges for Teacher Education, Denver, CO, March 2, 1985, p. 7.

[18]G. R. Anrig, "Identifying and Rewarding Excellence in Individuals." Panel Discussion at Annual Meeting of the Council of Chief State School Officers, Little Rock, AR, November 22, 1983, p. 3.

[19]Ibid.

[20]Anrig, "Teacher Education," p. 5.

[21]Ibid.

[22]T.A. Arciniega, "Equity, Access, and Quality Control Issues in Teacher Education." Speech presented to Summer Institute of the Council of Chief State School Officers, Delevan, WI, August 1, 1985, p. 2.

[23]Madrid, et al., p. 20.

[24]R. C. Schroeder, "Social Security Assessment." *Editorial Research Reports*, June 29, 1979, p. 468.

[25]J. McCue, "Baby Boom's New Echo." *Editorial Research Reports*, June 26, 1981, p. 485.

[26]Letter from H. L. Hodgkinson, January 23, 1986.

[27]Hodgkinson, *All One System*, p. 7.

[28]"The Disappearing Border." *U.S. News and World Report*. August 19, 1985, p. 30.

[29]Madrid, et al., p. 20.

[30]U.S. Department of Commerce, Bureau of Census, *Conditions of Hispanics in America Today*. Washington, D.C.: U.S. Government Printing Office, 1983, p. 13.

[31]"On El Main," p. 34.

[32]V. Burke, T. Gave, R. Rimkunas, J. Griffith, "Hispanic Children in Poverty." Washington, D.C.: Library of Congress, Congressional Research Service No. 85-170 RPW, September 13, 1985.

[33]Hodgkinson, *All One System*, p. 8.

[34]Madrid, et al., p. 31.

[35]Ibid., pp. 56-57.

[36]Ibid., pp. 58-59.

[37]J. Bruner, *In Search of Mind: Essays in Autobiography*. New York: Harper and Row, 1983, p. 196.

[38]K. F. McCarthy and R. B. Valdez, *Current and Future Effects of Mexican Immigration in California: Executive Summary*. Santa Monica: Rand Corporation, November, 1985.

[39]Ibid., p. 37.

[40]F. Newman, *Higher Education and the American Resurgence*. Princeton, NJ: Carnegie Foundation for Advancement of Teaching, 1985, p. xv.

[41]Letter from R. V. Padilla, January 23, 1986.

[42]R. V. Padilla and M. Montiel, "The Socio-Historical Context for Action," *An Action Plan for Chicano Higher Education in Arizona*. Tucson, AZ: Mexican American Studies and Research Center, University of Arizona, 1984. Compiled and edited for Arizona Association of Chicanos for Higher Education, pp. 9-10.

References

Anrig, G. R. "Identifying and Rewarding Excellence in Individuals." Panel discussion at Annual Meeting of the Council of Chief State School Officers, Little Rock, AR, November 22, 1983.

———. "Teacher Education and Teacher Testing: The Rush to Mandate." Speech to American Association of Colleges of Teacher Education, Denver, CO, March 2, 1985.

Arciniega, T. A. "Equity, Access, and Quality Control Issues in Teacher Education." Speech to Council of Chief State School Officers, Delevan, WI, August 1, 1985.

Astin, A. W. *Minorities in American Higher Education*. San Francisco: Jossey-Bass, 1982.

The Borderlands Journal 8:2, Spring, 1985.

Brown, G. H., N. L. Rosen, S. T. Hill, and M. A. Olivas. *The Condition of Education for Hispanic Americans*. National Center for Education Statistics, U.S. Department of Health, Education, and Welfare. Washington, D.C.: U.S. Government Printing Office, 1980.

Bruner, J. *In Search of Mind: Essays in Autobiography*. New York: Harper and Row, 1983.

Burke, V., T. Gave, R. Rimkunas, and J. Griffith. "Hispanic Children in Poverty." Washington, D.C.: Library of Congress, Congressional Research Service NO. 85-170 RPW, September 13, 1985.

Casso, H. J., and G. D. Roman, eds. *Chicanos in Higher Education: Proceedings of a National Institute on Access to Higher Education for the Mexican American.* Albuquerque: University of New Mexico Press, 1976.

College Board. "College Board Data Show Class of '85 Doing Better on SAT, Other Measure of Educational Attainment." News release, September 23, 1985.

Cohen, A. M. and F. B. Brawer. *The American Community College.* San Francisco: Jossey-Bass, 1982.

"Disappearing Border." *U.S. News and World Report*, August 19, 1985, pp. 30-42.

"Graying of America: Aging U.S. Population Poses Threat to Retirement Systems." *Congressional Quarterly Weekly Report*, March 17, 1979, p. 441.

Hodgkinson, H. L. *All One System: Demographics of Education, Kindergarten Through Graduate School.* Washington, D.C.: Institute of Educational Leadership, 1985.

_____. Personal correspondence, January 23, 1986.

Karabel, J. "Community College and Social Stratification." *Harvard Educational Review*, 42:4:521-562. November, 1982.

Ladman, J. R. "The U.S. Border Regional Economy: Interdependence, Growth, and Prospects for Change," in *Views Across the Border*, 2d ed., ed. S R. Ross (Albuquerque: University of New Mexico Press, in press).

Madrid, A., L. Estrada, R. Santos, and M. Tienda. *The Changing Profile of Mexican America: A Sourcebook for Policy Making.* Claremont, CA: Tomás Rivera Center, 1985.

McCarthy, K. F. and R. B. Valdez. *Current and Future Effects of Mexican Immigration in California: Executive Summary.* Santa Monica: Rand Corporation, 1985.

McCue, J. "Baby Boom's New Echo." *Editorial Research Reports,* June 26, 1981.

Newman, F. *Higher Education and the American Resurgence.* Princeton, NJ: Carnegie Foundation for the Advancement of Teaching, 1985.

Olivas, M. A. *The Dilemma of Access: Minorities in Two Year Colleges.* Washington, D.C.: Howard University Press, 1979.

Padilla, R. V. Personal correspondence, January 23, 1986.

_____, and M. Montiel, eds. *An Action Plan for Chicano Higher Education in Arizona.* Tucson, AZ: Mexican American Studies and Research Center, University of Arizona, 1984.

Santos, A. G. de los, Jr. "The Role of the Community College in Developing Hispanic Leadership," in *Hispanics in Higher Education: Leadership and Vision for the Next 25 Years,* ed. L. A. Valverde and S. B. García. Austin: Office for Advanced Research in Hispanic Education, University of Texas, 1982.

_____, J. Montemayor, and E. Solis, Jr. "Chicano Students in Institutions of Higher Education: Access Attrition, and Achievement." *Aztlán: International Journal of Chicano Studies Research*, 14;1;79-110. Spring, 1983.

Schroeder, R. C. "Social Security Assessment." *Editorial Research Reports*, June 29, 1979.

U.S. Department of Commerce. Bureau of Census. *Condition of Hispanics in America Today.* Washington, D.C.: U.S. Government Printing Office, 1983.

Vera, Ron. Personal correspondence, February 13, 1986.

NO LIMITS BUT THE SKY/
EL CIELO ES EL LIMITE

*W. Ann Reynolds**

I'm proud to have been invited to deliver the Tomás Rivera lecture by the Hispanic Caucus of the American Association for Higher Education.

If the 1960s was a decade of American campus growth and the 1970s one of campus unrest, the 1980s will surely be remembered as the decade of reports. The various commissions and reports now number close to one hundred. Those that have impinged closely on us in the California State University in the last six months are AASCU's National Commission on the Role and Future of State Colleges and Universities "To Secure the Blessings of Liberty" and the Carnegie Foundation for the Advancement of Teaching "College: The Undergraduate Experience in America." About to emerge is "Leaders for America's Schools" from the National Commission on Excellence in Educational Administration. Secretary Bennett has said that what is really wrong with us is that we charge too much relative to the quality of our product. How are we all, as educators, expected to make sense out of this babble?

Are we, as some would have us believe, in an "Irangate" with respect to educational success for our young people? Are they indeed learning too little and paying too much? Could it be we are not "competitive," the new buzz word (remember "meaningful" and "excellence")? Is the new panacea to be "assessment" or a "competency-based" curriculum? Should we all move to "performance funding"?

Whoa! Stop! I'd like to propose another approach: let's *simplify*.

Recall Father Guido Sarducci on "Saturday Night Live" and the five-minute college degree:

> Economics—supply and demand.
> Business—You buy and you sell it for more.
> Theology—Where is God? Everywhere. Why? Because he likes you.

That may be an extreme simplification but when faced with dogma from a hundred commissions, one becomes desperate. I do earnestly believe that we should move the educational process back into the hands of the willing doers—you in this audience. It is no longer fashionable to admit that I am a Benjamin Spock fan. The basic precept of his best-selling book on child-rearing was "You know more about it than you think you do." Thus encouraged, without a shred of instruction or experience, I waded into the care of a premature infant, taken home in this very city in a November snowstorm, weighing less than 5 pounds. She is now a fulsome lass of 19 and majoring in comparative literature. Her own intrinsic stamina plus Spock's clear practicality and *simplicity* made the difference. Admittedly, millions of women have been successful mothers over the centuries. But Spock guided the first generation of mothers in the '30s through the '60s who were rearing children in homes often far from those of their own mothers. In a simple way, he taught us good methods to keep

---

*The 1987 Tomás Rivera Lecture was presented at the National Conference on Higher Education of the American Association for Higher Education, Chicago, IL, March 2, 1987.

children well and reasonably content and, most important, lifted our own self-esteem in the process.

I should like to impose one brief and simple homework assignment, to be done in the next few days. Do not ponder the reports; do not re-review issues of the *Chronicle of Higher Education*. Instead, on the back of your airline ticket or a cocktail napkin, simplify and list your own thoughts about a college education. What do we do best? Where could we improve? What can I do, in a direct, practical way, to move the endeavor?

Let me give you a sample list of what colleges and universities have done well.

1. College attendance.   More than any nation in the world, we have provided a college opportunity for our young people. Our college-going rate increased from 40 percent of high school graduates in 1950 to 62.5 percent in 1983. In the same time span, high school graduation rates increased from 59 percent to 73 percent, a doubling of access to a college degree. Almost 20 percent of all Americans have achieved four years of college or more. Most of this growth in higher education has taken place since World War II. The decrease in college enrollments, predicted for the 1980s, because of the diminishing population of young people in the 18-to-25-year-old bracket, has not occurred because of a concomitant increase in their college-going rates.

However, this picture today has some storm clouds brewing overhead. The college-going rate in some states for black students has actually decreased and it is not increasing quickly enough for Hispanic students commensurate with their population cohort. The most ominous cloud of all is the diminishing Federal financial aid now available to students, resulting in reduced access and increased indebtedness at graduation.

2. Agricultural research.   Our agriculture schools have truly achieved a superb record in soil science, animal husbandry, crops, irrigation—all aspects of food production. These discoveries, almost all university-based, have revolutionized agriculture. Our nobility in exporting our techniques has enabled other nations to accumulate agricultural surpluses just like ours, with some devastating results for our own farm economy. Nevertheless, working so assiduously to enable all of the world's population to have adequate food to eat has been one of the finest accomplishments of mankind in this century.

3. Biomedical research.   The list here is prodigious and includes major advances in chemical and molecular genetics; radioimmunoassay of microblood constituents; understanding cellular receptors and the human immune system; organ transplantation; improved survival of low-birth-weight infants; *in vitro* fertilization and the identification of pituitary hormones.

Now let's turn to an equally brief, whimsical list of what we have *not* done well—but remember, we are trying to *simplify*.

1. International programs.   From the 1920s through the 1950s, our campuses made an extraordinary effort to move into international education, derived at first from missionary endeavors. With the emergence of the United Nations post-World War II, the effort reached its zenith and many institutions built large international houses where American students shared quarters as well as campus life with students from other countries. Most colleges planned and worked to have students from many nations enrolled with them. I was in college in the mid-1950s in Emporia, Kansas with students from Greece, Egypt, South America, Scandinavia and it even may count that we had a Hawaiian connection for our football team.

We collectively discarded that good record in the 1970s when we concentrated on foreign students characterized by a single trait—the abilities of their respective governments to pay for them. The balance tipped quickly to a preponderance of students from oil-rich countries and those students sent to us were mostly in engineering or other technical programs. Now we are back at our drawing boards, vigorously planning to recoup all that we managed to dissipate in the late 1960s and 1970s. In the West, we call it "Pacific Rim" planning and we have no time to lose. Meanwhile, we need to capitalize on the cultural and linguistic gifts brought to our campuses by our Hispanic and Asian students. At times, one weeps in despair. In California last fall, the electorate passed an "English only" initiative, a real slap at cultural values and diversity, while there is a backlog of thousands of people in Los Angeles desperately eager to take English courses. Why cannot our nation grasp that we should instead cherish and cultivate being bilingual and savor the richness of our various cultures?

2. Athletic programs.   Moving quickly, I come to our utter failure to manage major athletic programs on our campus. Enough said.

3. Socialization of male students.   As people who live next door to our campuses rush to point out to us, we have made precious little progress in our efforts to civilize male undergraduates, primarily those between the ages of 18 and 25. In the Old West, energies went into horses, cattle and an occasional gunfight or else the backbreaking drudgery of farming. Over the centuries, of course, fighting wars has been a horrible solution to the brash spirits of young men. Time is our ally. By the age of 30, most of these same young men are working with ties on, paying a mortgage and behaving like responsible husbands and fathers.

4. Representation of women and minorities.   Then, at a priority above all else, colleges and universities must do in the future what we have failed to do in the past, which is to involve women and minorities fully in the very core of our being. By that I mean the representation of women, Hispanics, Blacks, and Asians among our faculties, administrations and, critically, our student bodies should reasonably reflect their representation within the populations we serve. Dr. Tomás Rivera was a national leader in his determination to achieve this paramount goal. An education lifted him from the life of a migrant farm worker into a major university presidency. Tomás Rivera recognized that full human potential could only be achieved through education and was determined to apply his incredible talents to the goal of helping others achieve their potential—a goal I like to believe that he and I shared.

But to go back to my earlier premise—how can we marshal the resources we possess and work at what we can achieve? Instead of relying on global rhetoric, by thinking simply what can be done *now*? Because I know The California State University best, I shall use us as an example.

The California State University is the largest single educator of Hispanics in the nation. In 1984-85, nearly 3,000 Hispanics earned baccalaureate degrees on the 19 CSU campuses and nearly 25,000 were enrolled. About 10 percent of all Hispanics in the nation enrolled in four-year colleges are enrolled in CSU and about 14 percent of all Hispanic baccalaureate degree recipients in the nation complete their education in CSU. While CSU takes pride in the numbers of Hispanics it does educate, we are committed to increasing these numbers dramatically. El cielo es el límite.

We in California *must* do so if we are to serve our state and the nation. Some 5.7 million Hispanics live in California. By the year 2000 over one-fourth of our state's people will be Hispanic, and by 2030 38 percent of the state's population will be Hispanic. In California the Hispanic community is diverse. It includes Mexican Americans as well as immigrants from Mexico, Puerto Rico, and Central America. For the sake of brevity I am using the umbrella term, Hispanic, in full recognition that many different histories and cultures are represented in this group.

Our school population is increasingly made up of Hispanic young people. In 1985, about 42,000 of the public high school graduates in California were Hispanic, nearly 19 percent of the total. Today more than twice that number are in the ninth grade in California and nearly three times that number are enrolled in California first grades.

I want all of those first graders enrolled today to go to college should they choose. We simply must redouble our efforts to attract and to assure preparation for more and more Hispanic young people. We must have in our state and in the nation greater numbers of Hispanic businessmen and women, legislators, city council members, teachers, superintendents, lawyers, physicians, and nurses. Just to give you an idea of how far we have to go, Los Angeles, which has a population of over 816,000 Hispanics, in the last year elected its first Hispanic city council representative in more than 20 years and just recently elected a second. Only 6 percent of California's teachers are Hispanic, a far cry from the 29 percent of youngsters in grades K-12 who are Hispanic. Three percent of California's school superintendents are Hispanic. Nationally, only 2 percent of persons completing medical school and 2.5 percent of doctorate recipients are Hispanic (up from 1.2 percent in 1975).

In order to improve representation and success of Hispanics in The California State University, we have taken some practical steps over the last four years. In 1983, I appointed a Commission on Hispanic Underrepresentation, chaired by Dr. Tomás Arciniega, president of CSU Bakersfield. That group prepared a number of excellent recommendations. I am pleased to say that acting on several of these, the Trustees have requested and received nearly $12 million over the last several years to recruit and to retain more minorities in higher education. These include efforts to work with high minority intermediate schools to improve academic preparation, to improve orientation and introduction to the universities in Summer Bridge Programs, to support students deficient in basic skills and to improve teacher preparation.

Not everyone in this nation believes that there are no limits but the sky. Like many of you here, I am saddened by the diminution of what once was a firm commitment to equity in jobs and in education at the federal level. So many of the fine programs that led to gains in the numbers of college graduates from all minority groups in the 1960s and 1970s are gone or substantially reduced.

Even among those in the university community who agree that we must remain committed to the goals of educational equity as an end, there is disagreement as to the means. Some say we only must wait, that in time—maybe a century—representation of minority groups in education will improve. Others take an elitist approach—seeking to identify the most highly gifted youngsters from Hispanic and other backgrounds at an early age and either to remove them from barrio and ghetto schools or to isolate them within those schools to expose a select few to an enriched curriculum.

I think we must take a more aggressive, more simple and straightforward approach. I believe we must work to improve the schools that all youngsters attend, especially those whose students are predominately minorities, so that as many young people as possible keep open their option to go on to college. Of course, keeping options open means staying in school. Of all the problems facing education, the high proportion of students dropping out before completion of high school is the most troubling. In California, we estimate that almost one-quarter of whites, and one-third of Hispanics and blacks will drop out between the ninth and the twelfth grades. Many of those who do graduate are not prepared for college. Only 15 percent of Hispanic high school graduates in California in 1985 met regular admissions criteria for the CSU. Although many were admitted under special provisions, we know that the best chance for success and graduation lies with those who meet regular admissions criteria.

The Arciniega Commission report also indicated that the two biggest barriers to the success of Hispanic students in the CSU were lack of adequate financial support and inadequate preparation for college. To deal with the latter, we began a long process of defining and working with the public schools to implement a college-preparatory curriculum. This process has been risky and often misunderstood. What if the schools couldn't or wouldn't increase their academic offerings? Could this well-intentioned effort paradoxically become a barrier to the success of Hispanic students in high school? Just last week the analysis of high school preparation of our freshman class of 1986 was completed. Early data are most promising: The number of college preparatory courses taken by white students was unchanged while that of incoming Hispanic, black and Asian students had actually increased. The cumbersome process appears to be working for those young people who most need and are entitled to parity in preparation for college.

While we in the university tend to see education as the major vehicle for bringing more and more minorities into the mainstream of the American society, many minority youngsters and even their parents see schools and colleges as forbidding institutions, inhospitable to their aspirations. Let's face it—education has some negative images in the minds of many who have not experienced its more positive aspects. I want for us to think of several of them.

First, many young people from all groups are simply turned off by the surface features of schooling. Just a few weeks ago I hosted a meeting of community leaders from throughout the state. Included were the head of the Urban League in Los Angeles, the superintendent of a high minority school district, the executive director of the California branch of the American Medical Association, and the president of the Hispanic Business Association of California. At the conclusion of the meeting a young Hispanic woman who is a physician in California's Central Valley described how difficult it was to get teenage girls in a high school excited about going to college. When asked why, she gestured toward the wall of the room in which we were meeting at the system's office. On it were hanging photogtaphs of past presidents of the CSU Board of Trustees. There they were, 14 men and two women, only one ethnic minority—good people but not nearly as interesting to look at as Madonna, Bruce Springsteen, Tom Cruise, or Emilio Estévez.

Many of you in this room went to college at a time when there was no more interesting thing to do in the world but to learn about physics or Shakespeare or anthropology—this was especially true if you lived in rural America. I'm not so sure that that's the case today. Music videos, shopping malls, pink hair are on the face of it more fun than doing homework. But we all know the thrill of discovering how the universe works, the shock of recognizing our childhood emotions of fear dramatized in the characters in novels by Charles Dickens and Carlos Fuentes, or the pleasure of mastering even a phrase in a foreign language. First though, we had to get below the surface of routine classroom life to experience the joy of learning.

As a means of justifying education to many young people, instead of stressing the excitement of learning inherent in education, we have emphasized its practical value. Going to college is too often presented as something young people have to do before they can make lots of money. In the CSU about 30 percent of our students are enrolled in business or engineering programs. If you have to go, many people reason, you ought to choose what to study not because you want to study it, but because it holds the highest income potential. Thus, people who would enjoy being teachers or social workers sit doggedly through courses in accounting or computer science. Such mercenary values are often at odds with social and religious values that stress service to family and community.

We must not shrink from this recognition, many minority students experience overt and covert racism from fellow students, from staff, even from faculty. Think of the Hispanic student who never gets called on by the math professor even when she raises her hand. The professor thinks she won't know the answer and he won't know how to deal with her not knowing; soon she stops raising her hand and stops coming to class and loses interest in college.

Too many of us in the university do not see it as our responsibility to develop talent but only to identify and grade it. Some faculty seem to think they are graders and sorters, not teachers. A university is not an egg factory where people sit all day deciding if an egg is white or brown, large or extra large, A or AA, and plunking it into the right box. We *owe* our students a vigorous and engaging education.

One reason I am so heartened by the work of Professor Alexander Astin is that he reminds us that our job as educators is to develop the abilities of the persons who come to our colleges and universities. He urges us to measure our success by the talent we develop in students, not the abilities they have when they come to us. He reminds us that typically we think of the "best" schools as those that can attract from the outset the brightest students.

I have an acquaintance—I'm sure you know someone like him—who's had a terrible time establishing a career. He seems to move from job to job on a two-year cycle. I think it's because he just never got over going to Princeton! It's impossible for him to meet anyone without letting them know in the first three seconds that he went to Princeton.

Many of our young people are unwilling to become victims of the egg-grading and the status-seeking that they perceive is too much a feature of our universities.

I've been frank about some of the negative images minority young people and their families hold of higher education. But what are the alternatives?

Our colleges and universities are the only places where people can sample organized human knowledge. I want to borrow Matthew Arnold's definition of culture for my definition of education. "It is the best that has been known and said in the world" and thus represents "the history of the human spirit."

Even so, the university is not a library. It is a dynamic environment—faculty are defining new knowledge, students are bringing experiences to their learning that cause faculty to refine and to rethink their concepts and that cause other students to view knowledge in new ways.

At the same time the university gives students broad exposure to the world's knowledge; it gives them specialized skills that equip them to serve the business community or the public sector. We must not ignore preparation for employment in the university experience, but we must not let that become the driving force behind education in the minds of students.

I want to digress for a moment to speak to a concern I have about some national and state leaders who tend to think that we need only educate minority students in programs narrowly focused on job skills. In the minds of some, vocational education in community college is "enough" for a minority student. And even some minority parents think of the educational needs of their children in narrow terms. If women complete high school some parents think that is enough.

While college may not be for everyone, the chance to attend college and to complete a baccalaureate degree remains the primary means to fulfillment of personal, social, and economic potential. All of us must work to alter the negative images and realities universities afford many minority students. We need to speak up about the excitement of learning, the self-confidence that derives from mastering a tough subject.

We should remember too that as the number of minority students increases in our universities, some of the more negative features of education will be altered. There are already signs that the presence of minority students in classes is making faculty more conscious of the Eurocentrism of the curriculum.

On 11 of the 19 CSU campuses, faculty have participated in a project called Cross-Cultural Perspectives in the Curriculum. Interest in the project, now in its sixth year, is sustained by growing faculty acknowledgment that *what* we teach and *how* we teach are becoming increasingly remote from the social reality from which students come and in which they are likely to function in the future. Students from majority and minority cultures are inadequately exposed to the diversity of international, multicultural and gender perspectives, especially in their own and closely related fields of study.

With the assistance of specialists in intercultural communication, faculty attempt to understand how their communications are perceived by students of ethnic and cultural backgrounds different from their own. This understanding leads to changes that could make interaction with them in and out of class more supportive. Anecdotal evidence on the effectiveness of these efforts in modifying behaviors is encouraging.

Further evidence of change in the university is our attitude toward persons for whom English is not a first language. As CSU accepts more students of Hispanic and Asian backgrounds as entering freshmen, we are striving to recognize the benefit of having acquired two languages. We plan to assess the language skills of speakers of languages other than English and will recognize that achievement by declaring them exempt from the requirement of two years of study in high school.

While on the face of it such a policy seems entirely sensible, it is being resisted, sadly, by some of the very people whom we would expect to understand the value of learning languages other than English at an early age. Some foreign language teachers view formal classroom instruction as the only vehicle by which language acquisition can occur. We will be working both with current and prospective teachers to encourage more openness to second language speakers.

Such efforts to encourage new thinking among our faculty and in the policies of the university are recent. I want to give credit to those persons who were pioneers—who went to college and who graduated at a time when educational practices failed to recognize the needs of minority students. I like to believe that *state* colleges and universities have played a special role in the preparation of leaders from minority backgrounds.

The recently elected city councilman for Los Angeles, and former State Assemblyman, Richard Alatorre, is a 1965 graduate of Cal State Los Angeles. A leading California playwright, Luis Valdez, author of *Zoot Suit,* graduated from San Jose State in 1964.

CSU graduates are also increasingly assuming leadership in universities as faculty members and administrators. Carlos Muñoz, Associate Professor of Chicano Studies at UC Berkeley is a CSU alumnus. Cecilia Burciaga who graduated from CSU, Fullerton in 1967 is now Associate Dean for Graduate Studies at Stanford. Gloria Miranda who graduated from CSU, Dominguez Hills in 1971 is now Associate Professor of History at Los Angeles Valley College.

There are many others I could name and we salute them with great pride. We are determined to increase their numbers and thereby their influence.

I have listed many of the obstacles and some of the successes in our quest for appropriate educational attainment for Americans of Hispanic heritage. Many before me have done the same. It is a common academic exercise and often is followed by—nothing. What is perhaps most important in this quest is to try, to act, to take risks. Rash steps can be counterproductive, but thoughtful action is long overdue. The attempt that fails but provides the experience for a next and more effective step is progress.

I remember Chancellor Tomás Rivera with lovely clarity. Within a month of my coming to California, he journeyed to my office to welcome me, with that gentlemanly chivalry he possessed. He was the only higher education leader in the state to do so, incidentally. After a warm welcome, within fifteen minutes he had enlisted me in an organization he founded to promote greater involvement of minorities in higher education. Tomás, consider that you enlisted me for life—you started the warmest and most worthwhile call to service of my professional lifetime. Tomás Rivera's life was too short but as in genetics, he achieved a "multiplier effect" and his efforts surge forward.

His time in California was brief but he left a deep impression on many people in the state. Born to a family who lived as migrant workers, he earned an education and went on to become Chancellor of the Riverside campus of the University of California. He was the first person of Mexican American descent to be appointed Chancellor of a major research university.

His faith in education was great. In a letter to colleagues in 1984, he wrote, "A high quality of education provided at all levels for the Hispanic communities will ensure stronger individuals, and in turn, a stronger community. This type of education must be one of our constant and basic demands. We can only ensure this education if we lead, if we become involved in getting it, if we have trust in it, and most importantly, if we make it part of our prophecy."

The example of his life illustrates the truth of words in *Don Quixote,* "El cielo es el límite"—No limits but the sky. Thank you for allowing me to speak in his memory.

CALIFORNIA STATE UNIVERSITY

NOCIONES SOBRE EL ARTE NARRATIVO EN
"... *Y NO SE LO TRAGO LA TIERRA*"
DE TOMAS RIVERA

Teresa B. Rodríguez

Una de las razones por las cuales "... *y no se lo tragó la tierra*" constituye una novela cumbre en la narrativa chicana contemporánea es que su autor supo aprovechar las técnicas modernas en el arte de narrar, así construyendo una obra de realismo crítico. En ella se plantea con hondura la problemática social y existencial de un sector de la comunidad chicana: los trabajadores migratorios.

Los diversos elementos técnicos que convergen en *Tierra* revelan el afán del autor por conferirle a su obra una forma predeterminada. Es como si Rivera hubiese construído un molde en el cual vaciara el contenido amorfo de la novela.[1] Sin embargo, su preocupación por la forma no es gratuita, ya que en *Tierra*, la distancia que ha existido entre los dos elementos tradicionalmente antitéticos: *forma y contenido*, queda reducida considerablemente. En este sentido su concepción sobre el arte de novelar se acerca a la de Alain Robbe-Grillet, quien afirma que es justamente en la forma donde radican la realidad y el profundo significado de la novela.[2]

A primera vista *Tierra* aparece como una colección de cuentos (a la manera de *El llano en llamas* de Juan Rulfo), enlazados tenuemente por un intento de calar en la vida, y en los conflictos y las tribulaciones del pueblo chicano. El lector pronto descubre que los relatos poseen una fuerza de adherencia semejante a la que poseen las moléculas de un cuerpo. En este caso el cuerpo lo constituye la presencia del niño-protagonista en torno al cual se construye la dinámica de los diversos relatos. Hay catorce relatos, doce de ellos representan los meses del año, los otros dos, el primero y el último, forman un marco que da unidad a la novela. En el primero, "El año perdido", se presenta el conflicto de identidad del protagonista. En el último, "Debajo de la casa", el conflicto se resuelve. Salvo por "El año perdido", todos los demás relatos son antecedidos por una brevísima anécdota. Estas anécdotas son unidades narrativas en miniatura. Como los relatos, estas unidades narrativas presentan diversos fragmentos de existencia del pueblo chicano. En ellas se manifiesta un complejo de actitudes contradictorias por parte del narrador objetivo, o sea, el autor frente a su comunidad: distanciamiento e identificación, ironía y compasión, tragedia y humor, desesperanza y esperanza, enjuiciamiento de la sociedad dirigente y enjuiciamiento de la comunidad chicana.

Para propósitos de unidad y efecto estético, el autor experimenta con una técnica que se emplea a menudo en la poesía: diseminación y recolección. En "El año perdido" se presenta el protagonista. A través de los doce relatos y trece anécdotas hay una diseminación de personajes, conflictos y situaciones, que constituyen el grosor de la novela, y forman parte importante en la vida del protagonista, que de improviso, en el primer relato, despierta a una nueva concientización de sí mismo y de su pueblo. A través de los doce relatos recupera en su mente el año perdido. Al final, en "Debajo de la casa", las experiencias anteriores resurgen del subconciente y son recoleccionadas formando una síntesis regeneradora, por medio de la cual el protagonista encuentra su identidad. Esa experiencia marca el comienzo de un nuevo ser, que exhibe dos vertientes: la vida solitaria de un niño que siente profundamente y piensa con una mente crítica, y la vida gregaria de alguien que, a pesar de todo, se identifica con su pueblo del que se nutre cultural y espiritualmente. La alienación que inicialmente siente el protagonista queda anulada al final de la novela.

En *Tierra* la forma y el contenido se funden en el tratamiento del tiempo, que aparece como un recurso apropiado para los propósitos que persigue el autor. En el manejo de las múltiples variantes del tiempo en la novela—tiempo circular, tiempo fragmentado, tiempo estancado, distorsión del tiempo histórico, tiempo reversible en la memoria—Rivera se pone a la altura de la novela mundial, pero sobre todo de la novela hispanoamericana. Pongamos por caso: Asturias (*El Señor Presidente*), Fuentes (*La muerte de Artemio Cruz*), García Márquez (*Cien años de soledad*), Sábato (*El túnel*), Alejo Carpentier (*Los pasos perdidos*).

Sin limitarse a un comentario meramente sociológico respecto de la opresión económica que sufren los trabajadores agrícolas, Rivera manifiesta una actitud crítica ante la realidad de su propio pueblo chicano, y de la sociedad de la que el pueblo es víctima. Los relatos en conjunto son un testimonio de la vida ardua, con su trauma cotidiano, que viven los trabajadores migratorios. Las situaciones, presentadas con un realismo crudo, aunque no exento de humor y ternura, se enfocan desde diferentes perspectivas obligando al lector a forjarse su propio juicio sobre la realidad novelada. Por ejemplo, en "Los niños no se aguantaron", que marca el principio de la visión que tiene el protagonista en su esfuerzo por recobrar el año perdido, hay un narrador en tercera persona que relata un incidente de opresión económica que resulta en la muerte trágica de un niño. Con una economía asombrosa de palabras (característica de todos los relatos, dado que lo que no se dice cobra muchas veces tanta importancia como lo que se dice), se enfoca el incidente mismo, pero al final, hay un fragmento de diálogo entre dos compadres en el que se presenta otra perspectiva, y nos da la idea de que en un caso semejante salen perdiendo tanto los oprimidos como los opresores.

"Un rezo" es un monólogo dramático, o la oración intercesoria de una madre que ruega a Dios por su hijo, soldado que se encuentra perdido en acción. Su plegaria presenta la perspectiva cristiana, mientras que en la anécdota introductoria se retrata a una madre buscando consejo y seguridad en una mujer espiritista que intenta comunicarse con el espíritu del soldado extraviado.

"Es que duele" es una narración en primera persona. El niño-protagonista (que acaso sea el mismo de "El año perdido" y "Debajo de la casa") cuenta una experiencia que tuvo en la escuela que conduce a su expulsión. La ira y la frustración le impelen a golpear a un estudiante anglo que lo provoca hasta hacerlo explotar. Es una rebeldía abierta en contra de la violencia mental y emocional impuesta por la estructura de discriminación que impera en el ambiente escolar. El punto en cuestión es la educación del niño chicano. Se intercalan en la narración cinco retrocesos en forma de diálogos que iluminan otras facetas del asunto. Se desprenden, entonces, tres diferentes puntos de vista sobre la situación: La del niño-protagonista que se encuentra envuelto por un remolino de confusión y vergüenza, la de los padres del niño que sienten orgullo ante la asiduidad del hijo en las materias escolares, y la del director de la escuela que cultiva actitudes racistas y nociones estereotipadas acerca de los chicanos. Estas diversas facetas que se presentan, en toda la novela y en muchos de los relatos, le confieren a *Tierra* una técnica cubista, ya que una determinada realidad se ve desde varios ángulos.

La novela de Rivera es un ejemplo del subgénero *Bildungsroman*, por cuanto traza el desarrollo de un niño. Pertenecen también a esta categoría otras novelas chicanas como *Pocho, Bless Me, Ultima* y *Barrio Boy*. El desarrollo del niño en Tierra es también multi-facético. En su desenvolvimiento como ser humano, surgen experiencias traumáticas, trágicas, o en ocasiones placenteras, tanto en su propia vida como en la de la comunidad.

Estas experiencias inevitables dejan huellas, a veces para bien, a veces para mal, en la vida interior del niño.

Como "El rezo", "La mano en la bolsa" es un monólogo dramático, pero esta vez, no es una mujer sino el niño-protagonista el que narra; y el que escucha no es Dios sino, al parecer, un compañero del protagonista. Se establece un contraste violento entre la inocencia del niño y la conducta homicida de la pareja, Don Laíto y Doña Bone, quienes lo hospedan en su casa con el propósito de que termine el año escolar mientras sus padres trabajan en el campo. El niño no sólo se convierte en testigo mientras sus tutores asesinan a un trabajador mexicano indocumentado, sino que además se hace cómplice, puesto que él cava la fosa y ayuda a sepultar el cadáver. Esta experiencia, que va más allá de lo doloroso y trágico hasta tocar los bordes de lo grotesco y horripilante, es un paso más en el proceso de desarrollo que experimenta el protagonista. Al verse involucrado en un crimen de tamaña dimensión, el niño se llena de temor y culpabilidad, experiencia vital que lo conduce a la pérdida de su inocencia.

Acaso podría afirmarse que el niño-protagonista es el autor mismo, quien a través de su personaje, valora su propia comunidad y destaca las rémoras sociales y espirituales para abrir la posibilidad hacia una renovación cultural. Esta actitud crítica se manifiesta sobre todo en "La noche estaba plateada", y en el relato central ". . . y no se lo tragó la tierra". En ambos el niño-protagonista se revela en contra de nociones establecidas por la tradición que otros se atreven a poner en tela de juicio. Para el protagonista la opresión no sólo se impone desde afuera sino desde adentro. Es decir, el racismo y la explotación económica contra el pueblo chicano no es el único muro que le impide caminar hacia el progreso. Desde la perspectiva del protagonista, el pueblo también se autooprime y se convierte en víctima de sí mismo mediante nociones retrógradas respecto a la religión y a la existencia del bien y del mal. Cuando el protagonista se rebela en contra de toda una manera de pensar, crece su distanciamiento entre él y su propia comunidad, pero él experimenta un sentido de liberación y al final de cuentas ese distanciamiento entre él y los suyos disminuye.

Para destacar esta condición en ambos relatos, "La noche estaba plateada" e ". . . y no se lo tragó la tierra", el autor emplea un acercamiento bifocal. Así se establece el contraste entre las ideas audaces del protagonista y las creencias convencionales de sus mayores. Sin embargo, en ". . . y no se lo tragó la tierra" la actitud crítica del protagonista es mucho más intensa que en "La noche estaba plateada," ya que el conflicto del relato se centra en el sufrimiento humano causado por la explotación económica y los afectados directamente son los miembros de su propia familia. En "La noche estaba plateada" las acciones del niño-protagonista las motiva su mente inquisitiva, mientras que en ". . . y no se lo tragó la tierra" sus emociones son encauzadas por un sentido de justicia frente al dolor de los oprimidos. El niño encarna la misma actitud y plantea la misma pregunta intemporal de Job, el patriarca del Antiguo Testamento: "¿Por qué sufren los justos, y los malos prosperan?"[3] Observa cómo las labores arduas del campo han consumido a su tía y han dejado a su tío inservible, con tuberculosis, y el muchacho se llena de rabia ante las circunstancias. Por otra parte, su madre adopta una actitud de resignación, arguyendo que el sufrimiento es una experiencia inseparable de la vida humana en conformidad con la voluntad de Dios, la cual acepta de una manera estoica. Su hijo no sólo pone en duda la eficacia de la fe religiosa, sino que maldice a Dios abiertamente después de que su padre y hermano menor sufren un colapso en el trabajo. Mientras que su madre espera con mansedumbre la promesa de la recompensa celestial, el hijo se llena de ira y desesperación al no poder encontrar la manera de cambiar las circunstancias inmediatas. Afirma que la fe religiosa de su madre tiende a convertirse en una forma de esclavitud que conduce al fracaso.

Narrado en primera persona, "Primera comunión" marca ya otra etapa importante en el desarrollo del niño. Desde el principio el narrador protagonista hace esta observación: "Yo siempre recordaré aquel día en mi vida".[4] Se refiere al día en que sufrió una experiencia traumática al despertar abrupta e inesperadamente al misterio de la sexualidad humana. En este relato hay también un dualismo en el enfoque: La visión interna del narrador y la perspectiva externa del medio que lo rodea. Acosado por su hogar y la iglesia, el niño es arrojado a un estado de confusión con respecto al significado del pecado y la condenación eterna. Ambos ambientes le inculcan un temor malsano. Su madre coloca un retrato del infierno en la cabecera del niño y decora la habitación con imágenes fantasmagóricas. En la clase de catecismo la monja—obsesionada con el sexo—hace que los niños reciten y ensayen los pecados de la carne, una y otra vez, en preparación para la primera comunión. El trauma ocurre cuando el protagonista se asoma por la ventana de la sastrería contigua a la iglesia y descubre a una pareja desnuda haciendo el amor en el piso. Queda paralizado de terror momentáneamente. Más tarde se da cuenta de lo que la monja quería decir por los pecados de la carne. La experiencia permanece gravada en su mente, la confusión aumenta y al final del relato dice: "Tenía ganas de saber más de todo. Y luego pensé que a lo mejor era lo mismo" (p. 64).

"Los quemaditos" es un ejemplo de ironía sutil. El sueño de una familia de trabajadores migratorios que anhelan romper el ciclo de miseria y opresión se convierte en una trágica pesadilla cuando dos niños mueren quemados. Los guantes de boxear son el símbolo de esperanza de que algún día uno de los niños llegue a convertirse en un gran boxeador y rescate a la familia de la miseria económica. Sin embargo, si no hubiese sido por los guantes de boxear no se habría producido la tragedia. En su estructura narrativa "Los quemaditos" es casi idéntico a "Los niños no se aguantaron". En ambos relatos la narración en tercera persona se alterna con fragmentos de diálogos, y aunque el niño-protagonista no aparece en ninguno de los dos, de alguna manera asimila esas experiencias.

En "La noche que se apagaron las luces" el amor no correspondido conduce al suicidio. Hay una perspectiva múltiple en la que interviene brevemente al principio y al fin el narrador en tercera persona. Otros puntos de vista los dan dos observadores de la acción, amigos de Ramón. Hay diálogos entre Ramón y Juanita, una carta a Juanita de parte de Ramiro (la tercera persona que integra el triángulo amoroso), monólogos de Juanita y Ramón. Cada punto de vista es como la pieza indispensable de un rompecabezas, que visto en su totalidad presenta el objeto en todas sus dimensiones. El narrador en tercera persona da la perspectiva externa y los personajes revelan la encadenación de eventos que conduce a Ramón a su autodestrucción. Al igual que en otros relatos, hay una distorsión del tiempo cronológico entre cambios abruptos del espacio narrativo.

"La noche buena" es una narración en tercera persona. El autor inserta fragmentos de diálogos y monólogos con el propósito de presentar otras facetas de la situación que se narra. El conflicto opera en torno a la lucha infructuosa de una madre por sobreponerse a sus síntomas de neurastenia y el sentimiento de inseguridad entre gente desconocida por amor a sus hijos. En su precaria condición, caminar de casa al centro de la ciudad constituye una proeza increíblemente valerosa. Sus esfuerzos, sin embargo, son frustrados cuando se ve arrollada por los nervios y pierde el sentido de orientación entre la muchedumbre. Aturdida, sale de la tienda. La sigue un policía anglosajón; ella ajena al hecho de que se le ha olvidado pagar por los juguetes que quería comprar. El policía la acosa, y ella pierde el conocimiento. Al final, se advierten cuatro perspectivas diferentes: 1) la de ella—que se percibe a sí misma como persona inútil, incapaz de suplir las necesidades de sus hijos—, 2) la del policía—en quien resaltan el odio y los prejuicios raciales—, 3) la del marido—quien trabaja de lavaplatos dieciocho horas diarias y carece de tiempo para ir de compras con su mujer, y que se resigna a decir que al fin y al cabo es mejor tener esperanza—y 4) la de los niños—que sin poder asimilar la situación familiar en todas sus ramificaciones, entienden lo suficiente para no exigir que se les compren regalos de Navidad.

Un niño—al parecer el protagonista de la novela—aparece en "Retrato", pero esta vez no es el personaje central. Se sitúa en la perspectiva de testigo. Su intervención es muy breve, puesto que la mayor parte del relato la constituyen fragmentos de diálogos. El narrador ofrece una perspectiva general, externa, mientras que las cualidades esenciales de los personajes se revelan mediante las confrontaciones que tienen unos con otros mediante la técnica del *showing*. El diálogo destaca el contraste entre los sutiles ardides del inescrupuloso vendedor de retratos y la determinación que toma don Mateo, quien aparece demasiado crédulo al principio, y después es movido por un sentido de justicia y por las heridas que ha sufrido su autoestima al ser engañado de una manera tan insidiosa.

Uno de los relatos mejor logrados en cuanto a la forma es "Cuando lleguemos", en el que se advierte un afán por calar en lo más profundo de la conciencia colectiva de los trabajadores migratorios. El relato está estructurado sobre una multiplicidad de voces. Hay una perspectiva externa dada por el narrador en tercera persona, que hace una intervención al principio y otra al final del relato, confiriéndole así un marco dentro del cual se desarrollan quince monólogos. Esta estructura sirve para que quince personajes anónimos, que a su vez se convierten en narradores, revelen su problemática personal. Del conjunto de monólogos, se desprenden importantes nociones acerca de las tribulaciones, las esperanzas, los sueños de la gente—que sobrevive a fuerza de una lucha constante dentro de una estructura social opresora. La situación que se plantea es la siguiente: Un camión de carga que transporta a un grupo de trabajadores y sus familias de Texas a Minnesota se descompone inesperadamente a las altas horas de la noche. Los trabajadores se recogen dentro de sí mismos, coleccionan sus pensamientos y reflexionan sobre su condición, mientras esperan la incertidumbre del nuevo día. En este relato, como en otros, Rivera hace patente sus dotes de narrador en la manera en que se manipula el punto de vista.

Como hemos señalado, los doce relatos representan fragmentos de la experiencia vital del protagonista. El autor experimenta con la técnica de fragmentación y dislocación, permitiéndole al lector activarse en la reconstrucción de la realidad narrada. Así, el lector asume la misma función del protagonista cuando éste se encuentra "Debajo de la casa"; es decir, hace una recolección con el fin de crear una síntesis explicativa. Una vez más, en este último relato encontramos un doble enfoque. El narrador en tercera persona presenta la perspectiva externa, mientras que a través del fluir de la conciencia del protagonista asistimos a un proceso de interiorización. Experiencias sepultadas en el subconsciente surgen al nivel de la conciencia en forma desordenada hasta que se realiza la síntesis regeneradora que marca el final de la recuperación simbólica del año perdido. Así, el protagonista encuentra su lugar dentro de su propia comunidad de la cual se sintió alienado en diversos momentos de su existencia.

Acaso valga comparar "*. . . y no se lo tragó la tierra*" con un mural gigantesco. El autor logra a través de la palabra lo que el pintor crea sobre un muro. Es decir, toma todos los elementos de una experiencia, los fragmenta por completo—creando lo que Picasso llamaría "destrucciones"[5]—para después reordenarlos de tal manera que surge una nueva síntesis al final: "la suma de las destrucciones".[6] "*. . . y no se lo tragó la tierra* ha quedado como un hito dentro de nuestra novela contemporánea, entre otras razones, por la forma novedosa con que se plantea la problemática de un sector importante del pueblo chicano.

UNIVERSITY OF NORTHERN COLORADO

Notas

[1]La obra de Rivera es de género ambiguo, pues si juzgamos desde la perspectiva de la relación entre contenido y estructura, "... *y no se lo tragó la tierra*" puede considerarse o una colección de cuentos o una novela. Consideramos, sin embargo, que *Tierra* se acerca más al concepto de novela.

[2]Alain Robbe-Grille, *For a New Novel: Essays on Fiction*. Translated by Richard Howard (New York: Grove Press Inc., 1965) 43.

[3]Véase el capítulo 21 del libro de Job.

[4]Tomás Rivera, "... *y no se lo tragó la tierra*" (Berkeley: Editorial Justa Publications, 1977) 58. Referencias subsiguientes aparecerán incorporadas al cuerpo de este ensayo entre paréntesis.

[5]Hugh C. Holman, *A Handbook to Literature* (Indianapolis: The Odyssey Press, 1976) 143.

[6]Ibid.

RITUAL AND RELIGION IN TOMAS RIVERA'S WORK

Santiago Daydí-Tolson

It is probably impossible to discuss Tomás Rivera's contributions without having to deal, at one point or another, with the subject of ritual and religion. Either in relation to the author's direct or allusive treatment of religious aspects of Chicano customs, or in relation to stylistic and structural resonances of religious texts and rituals in the literary work, Rivera's critics have to confront the fact that religion has a significant presence in the author's writings and plays an important part in his literary representation and intellectual interpretation of Chicano consciousness and worldview. Many instances of ritual and religion interact and combine themselves in most of Rivera's writings, creating a structuring pattern of motives. Their persistence and poignancy call immediate attention to their possible meanings and functions within a given text and, more so, within the framework of the wider, complete outlook communicated by the author through his different works—articles, poems and narratives.

As he was convinced that literature could "give form, harmony and unity to Chicano life,"[1] Tomás Rivera took special interest in representing in his literary works a complete view of the Mexican-American culture and of the Chicano experience.[2] In such representation religion has preeminence and becomes one of the most important factors in the analysis of the unique Chicano worldview. The author is well aware that ritual, religion and the sacred are central to the Mexican-American mind and have a profound effect on Chicano life and ideology. As Sylvia S. Lizárraga has observed in reference to religion in ". . . *y no se lo tragó la tierra*," "Rivera muy atinadamente ha encontrado cuál es la fuerza central de donde emanan las influencias que condicionan nuestra manera de pensar y consecuentemente nuestra manera de comportarnos en toda situación en que nos encontremos."[3] It has to be added, also, that regardless of the ideological views of the Chicano author and intellectual, the old traditional religious conceptions and values inherited from the Mexican culture play an important role in the acquisition of his own views and interpretations.

The treatment of religion in Rivera's stories is directed mainly towards a critical repudiation and disavowal of religious beliefs and habits among his people. The author does not deal with religion as a positive spiritual force, but as a form of psychological limitation to the social advancement of the Mexican American. He refers to religion in mostly negative terms, either using irony and humor, or just by contrasting in simple images the absurdity of religious beliefs with the practical, logical forms of everyday life. Such criticism touches as much the abstract notion of God and the sacred as the concrete reality of religion as a cultural and social institution. Rivera's critical attitude clashes with the traditional religious views among Mexican Americans: the profound conviction about the authority and power of God, and the accepting and resigned attitude in the face of life's miseries and human shortcomings. In this respect, Rivera represents a new attitude among Mexican Americans, a breaking away from the traditional worldview of the people he is trying to portray. But even this being the case, the new attitude, manifest in the short stories of ". . . *y no se lo tragó la tierra*," does fit the reality of the Mexican American group the writer is dealing with.

The critical view of traditional religious values and customs represents the acculturation of the younger generations, the moving away of Chicano youth from the traditional world of their parents and Mexican ancestors towards a modern, less naïve understanding of their socio-cultural reality. The impact of the educational process on the young among the Mexican migrant groups results in their being able to look critically at their families' and community's religious views, and to challenge them with a different, more humanist attitude towards their world. For Rivera, as for most Chicanos at the moment when he began publishing his works, the objective of his writing was to generate change, to call for a new sense of identity for the Mexican American. That this change meant the apparent contradiction of embracing tradition and at the same time imposing a new reasoning based in more contemporary philosophical and ideological modes is indicative of the difficult process by which a people must reach a sense of uniqueness within a new cultural environment. In this sense, Rivera's reference to ritual and religious values among Mexican Americans is one of the central aspects of his originality as a Chicano writer responsible for the establishment of a Chicano consciousness.

In his article "La embestida contra la religiosidad en ". . . *y no se lo tragó la tierra*," Juan Rodríguez has demonstrated how religion is central to a sociological interpretation of Rivera's book as a truly revolutionary Chicano work. By so doing he has established the basic function of religion in Rivera's work: to make manifest the Chicano rebellion against the established social powers which dominate and subjugate Mexican Americans, hampering their possibilities for modernization and social adaptation within the frameworks of an alien society.[4] Rivera himself alludes to this interpretation of his writings when he observes: "¿Qué tiene de pasivo maldecir a Dios? La frustración del pueblo se incrementa adentro de ellos por la toma de conciencia sobre su situación económica y social, estallando en contra de sus creencias culturales sin condenar la sociedad."[5] In spite of the plural reference to the people in this citation, the rebellious attitude does not appear in Rivera's writings as a reaction of the whole community, but as the personal bearing of only one individual who is shown in clear contrast to the group.

The boy, who can be seen as the central character of ". . . *y no se lo tragó la tierra*," appears as a loner who defies the belief and customs of his people. If the unidentified boy represents the collective mind of the group, it could be suggested that he does not constitute a truly individual character, but the representation of a whole generation. Rivera himself uses the singular to refer to the collective when he talks about the Chicano in general and says that "this is the type of character I tried to portray in my work."[6] And since there is no clear indication in the literary text that the different voices and characters of the child protagonist in most of the stories are one and the same, it is also possible to add that the young character is not identified by name because it is not an individual figure but a collective figure of the young Chicano who has come to terms with the social conditions of his people.[7] Rivera is purposely ambiguous with respect to the identity of his main characters in ". . . *y no se lo tragó la tierra.*" Besides, in his critical essays he talks about several boys—"I deliberately used in my work young characters or children for the most part"[8]—, but at the same time he suggests the individuality of the character —"the child remembers and discovers."[9] In a sense, he is pointing to the difficult situation of the young Chicano in his becoming aware of his identity as an individual and as a member of a clearly defined group within American society.

This conflict of identification is a crucial aspect in Rivera's analysis of his people. As a motif it is present in several of his writings, as, for instance, in the poem "Always," from *Always and Other Poems.*[10] By using the second person singular, Rivera underlines in this poem the basic motif of personal identification in the recognition of the other; the individual sees himself in the rest of men, and in the measure that he knows and understands those who surround him he is able to know and to understand himself. The poem condenses in a dramatic image the idea Rivera has expressed in one of his critical writings: [11]

> You have seen yourself
> for you have been looking
> out the door
> Always

"Looking out the door" is a perfect image to express the duality of self and other, of interior life and outside world. This symbolic scene of the poem finds its equivalent in the scene of the last segment of ". . . *y no se lo tragó la tierra*"—"Debajo de la casa"[12]—in which a boy looks at the street from under the house. This situation represents the perfect haven for the individual who is considering his own situation with respect to the world and requires at the same time the loneliness to think by himself, and the proximity to others which keeps him aware of his social ties.

In the narrative text the loneliness of the character could be interpreted as a natural stage in the individual's development towards a final encounter with his collective destiny, which is represented by the waving of the arm from atop a tree, and by the desire to embrace all of the people he remembers: "Quisiera ver a toda esa gente junta. Y luego si tuviera unos brazos bien grandes los podría abrazar a todos" (p. 168). As suggested by Juan Rodríguez, this stage of loneliness represents a transition that, in terms of the rite of passage, constitutes a required step in the process of maturation: "One of the most important characteristics of the hero of an *Erziehungsroman* is that in the process of initiation and education in life he must separate himself from his group."[13] In the poem this condition of separateness acquires the attribute of permanence, as indicated by the title itself—"Always"—and by its repetition after each stanza. It is by virtue of this permanence that the individual becomes part of a collective mind. The second stanza again offers a clear coincidence with a section from ". . . *y no se lo tragó la tierra*," this time the one at the beginning "El año perdido" (p. 1), in which the speaker expresses his difficulties in knowing himself:

> You never sleep
> never dream
> You wait for yourself
> Always

The poem closes with a reinforcement of the idea that the individual is a mere representation of the whole group, even in the wide chronological spread of ancestral time:

> You have seen yourself
> You were here before
> many
> yesterday
> today
> ever
> behind the door
> Always

The different narrative points of view used in ". . . *y no se lo tragó la tierra*" also function as a means to communicate this collective sense of identity. The contrast between the individual and the group has to be considered in terms of historical change, of a transformation in Chicano contemporary life. The poem does not include this historically defined aspect; it only stresses the identity of all members of a community through time and the understanding of this fact by the individual. The different treatment of the same motif in two separate works should not be read as a contradiction in Rivara's ideas, but only as a means of stressing different aspects of the same complex motif. After all, in "*. . . y no se lo tragó la tierra*" the deep sense of community that unites the individual to the group pervades all texts and even defines the central theme of the book. The added element of change through rebellion against traditional values does not deny this sense of belonging; on the contrary, because of it the rebellious attitude acquires a socially desirable value.

The reaction of the individual against the common attitude of the group is found in another of Rivera's poems, "Siempre el Domingo."[14] Although one could read in this poem "the sense of being alone within a group,"[15] the sense of belonging to such a group is still a stronger feeling and dominates the poem's view. The clearly expressive images of the poem reinstate the idea that the generational difference between the old people—old not only in the sense of age—and the new Chicanos, aware of their choices, matters as much as the sense of belonging to a group. The contrast between "they" and "I" is established in the two first stanzas, although it is somewhat counteracted by the use of Spanish, the language that represents the essence of belonging to the group and partaking of the tradition:

> Vayan a la iglesia el domingo
> y rueguen por yo pecador,
> mientras,
>
> yo veo la ametralladora japonesa
> y las paracaídas alemanas
> y las banderas italianas
> y los retratos de tantos hombres muertos
> en *Veteran's Place.*

The two opposing locales—the church and the Veteran's Place—represent two forms of the temple, the place for public rituals and ceremonies. At this first stage in the poem, the opposition is not as clear as in the next stanza, where the sacramental view of a war museum or memorial for the heroes (not too different from the old churches with their tombs and mausoleums) is denied its sacred ceremonial status by moving the place of emotional communion with the dead from the room of worship to the bar:

> ¡Que me hallen allí en la cantina!
> ¡Que miren las bayonetas
> y las banderas
>   y a Villa
>   y a Pershing
>   y a Obregón
>   y a Ike
>   y a Carranza
>   y a mi cuate
>   y a todos esos hombres muertos
> en las guerras!
>
> ¡Que nos miren bailar!
> ¡Que miren que vivimos
> como ellos lo quisieran!

The change in the speaker's voice from the first person singular used in most of the poem to the first person plural in one short stanza might cause some confusion in the interpretation of the text, particularly because the idea of an opposition between the group and the individual was so clearly established in the previous stanzas. This seemingly inconsistent use of the pronouns can be understood only by seeing a communion of the single speaker with the dead soldiers revived in the ceremony of celebration. The group of churchgoers—the majority of people—is now opposed and challenged in its values not only by a single dissident, but by the larger group of dead heroes, the martyrs of society and saints of this civil sanctuary.

The direct stylistic allusion to the enumerative prayers in the mass at the memento of the dead, with its gradation from the historical figures to the most immediate friends and relatives and finally to the whole of society, enhances the effect of comparison or, better yet, of disparity between both rituals. While in church, prayers are said for the dead and for the living who someday will be united with the former in death; at the bar in the *Veteran's Place* the ceremony is more like a party, in which the living are trying to bring back to life with drinking and dancing those who are dead. If at the beginning of the poem one could have thought of a simple exchange of locales from one type of temple to another, at the end the opposition is much more drastic and telling. In both cases one has to recognize the ritual and its social function:

Vayan a la iglesia y recen por su salvación.
Yo me voy
a la cantina
a bailarles y
divertirles
a tantos hombres muertos
mientras,
las botellas regurgitan.

The division is now complete: The churchgoers are not asked to pray for the "I sinner," but for themselves. The dissident speaker has broken completely with the church and is celebrating his own civic ritual.

Besides confirming the author's critical view of religion, "Siempre el domingo" points to an important aspect in Rivera's thought that certainly requires more critical attention: his interpretation of Chicano literature as a ceremonial ritual, as a "Fiesta of the Living,"[16] a concept he must have developed in part from his reading of Octavio Paz. Like many Chicanos of his generation, Rivera used *El laberinto de la soledad* as a source of inspiration and as a means to approach for the first time the question of Chicano identity.[17] Rivera opens his article "Chicano Literature: Fiesta of the Living" with an epigraph from Octavio Paz's *El laberinto de la soledad*: "Every poem we read is a recreation, that is, a ceremonial ritual, a fiesta." ("Cada poema que leemos es una recreación, quiero decir: una ceremonia ritual, una Fiesta").[18] In his essay Octavio Paz develops a theory of the Mexican Fiesta, which Tomás Rivera takes very much into account when he develops his concept of Chicano literature as a "Fiesta of the living," as well as when he deals with religion in his writings.

Essential to Paz's concept of Fiesta is the idea of ritual, as the Fiesta is in itself a ritual, as much as the Mass, the individual prayer, and the First Communion—all of them present in Rivera's literary works—are rituals. In "Todos santos, día de muertos" (pp. 42-58), the third chapter of his *Laberinto de la soledad*, Paz develops his theory about the Fiesta and establishes the ritualistic quality of Mexican life. The rituals and ceremonies so abundant in Mexico are not necessarily religious in context, but they are well within the realm of the sacred. The Fiesta is a participation. This concept in particular is taken by Rivera in his interpretation of Chicano literature as participation, a communion of all writers and Chicanos in the discovery of their own social self. He writes:

> For me the literary experience is one of total communion, an awesome awareness of the "other," of one's potential self. I have come to recognize my "other" in Chicano literature, but by this I do not mean to say that I find or reflect or faithfully render the Chicano experience. . . . Rather, I would like to focus on Chicano writing as a ritual of immortality, of awe in the face of the "other"—a ritual of the living, in a sense, a fiesta of the living.[19]

This conception certainly cannot be termed religious in spite of all its proximity to a religious view of reality, although it is clear that for Rivera Chicano literature touches the sacred aspect of human life when it "reveals the Chicano as a complete person." As he explains, "inner sensitivity, self invention, remembering and discovery are personal processes. All this is something sacred. And it is ours."[20] The terms "sacred" and "ours" are closely related to his understading of literature as a ritual of discovery and participation. As for the term "ritual," it is important to observe that Rivera repeats it several times in "Chicano Literature: Fiesta of the Living," when discussing the value of literature for himself and for the Chicano. Thus, he has found Chicano writers "to be truthful, ritualistic, in love with the 'other' which each of them has found" (p. 19). Naturally, he thinks that through literature "we must return to the direct experience of life and our need for ritual" (p. 20), the need for creating bonds. The sense of belonging to a group is then a "sense that we are part of the same ritual" (p. 21); consequently, literature acquires a ritual function: "We must ritualize our existence through words" (p. 21). For Rivera all literature is a "ritual of remembering" and Chicano literature "is a ritual from which to derive and maintain a sense of humanity—a ritual of cleansing and a prophecy" (p. 22).

The religious terminology is too evident to be dismissed as purely coincidental. The author is applying it to literature as a means to communicate his faith in the power of art, a power and effectiveness akin to that of religion and religious rituals. For Octavio Paz, the idea of the sacred and of religious rituals is tied to his wider philosophical views and permeates his interpretations of culture, poetry and the arts. That is not the case with Rivera, whose basic philosophical views seem to be much nearer to a positivistic pragmatism probably of Anglo inspiration. It is obvious, though, that for him the negation of the established religious tradition required some form of substitution in order to be able to deal with the sacred and ceremony, and this substitution was provided by literature. In a reflection on his younger years the author comments:

> I dropped out of the Catholic Church at about fourteen—not dropped out, really, I just didn't want to have anything to do with religion right then. By the time of high school graduation I was reading about religion and I became pretty cynical. Well, Walt Whitman was my replacement: 'I sing the body electric.' Powerful things like that.[21]

That poetry became the substitution for religion should prove that from very early in his intellectual and emotive development the writer was taking a humanist stand that in all probability was the result of his education.

The "powerful" poetic images constituted for the young writer a new language that, in turn, lead to a new understanding of the personal circumstance. At this point it is important to observe that his choice of Walt Whitman, the writer who substituted poetry for religion, matters mainly because in Rivera's own work the sense of ritual and of the sacred communion of all men, the Fiesta of the poetic communication, is highlighted successfully. The term "powerful" used by Tomás Rivera in reference to Whitman's poetry also points to the true quality of the substitution. Poetry, the ceremonial ritual with mysterious and even sacred undertones, became the new form of linkage with the other. Later in his life he would be able to establish a similar linkage with other Chicanos, thus making the ritual of poetry a much more fascinating Fiesta because of its significance in term of the communion with those who up to that moment were absent or unknown to the writer:

> At twelve, I looked for books by my people, by my immediate people, and found very few. Very few accounts in fact existed. When I met Bartolo, our town's itinerant poet, and when on a visit to the Mexican side of the border, I also heard of him. . . . I was engulfed with *alegría*. It was an exaltation brought on by the sudden sensation that my own life had relationships, that my own family had relationships, that the people I lived with had connections beyond those at the conscious level.[22]

The biographical fact of having lost interest in the teachings of the Catholic Church at fourteen years of age, two years after the discovery of another type of ritual, is not enough to explain why the character who denies the existence of God in ". . . *y no se lo tragó la tierra*" is a child. Regardless of the psychological probabilities of a loss of religious faith in puberty, the age of the protagonist has particular significance for Rivera. In "Remembering, Discovery and Volition in the Literary Imaginative Process" he addresses the subject of children as literary characters, and declares: "I deliberately used in my works young characters or children for the most part" (p. 71). The reasons for this preference are summarized in the observation that all children are discoverers and the Chicano child "is a true Columbus:"

> The Chicano child, as every man in his particular surroundings, discovers certain realities—family, language, things about himself. He also discovers family relationships, the teachings of the Church. In sum, he is presented with his culture, a culture he assimilates, reconstructs, and in which he lives. Later on, he learns about relationships between towns and *barrios*. Still later, when he least expects it, he is presented with the reality of American ideology. Not that he had not perceived it previously but he had seen that whole world as a film—real but not real, a vicarious experience. In this way, the child comes by the discovery of America.[23]

These words not only present a blueprint of the essential themes of ". . . *y no se lo tragó la tierra*" and their relationship with ritual and religion, but they also point to the significance of Rivera's narrative within the context of Latin American literature. As it has been observed, ". . . *y no se lo tragó la tierra*" might well be considered as an example of a narrative of youth or a ritual of passage. As such, and corroborating the observations about the character's identity made before, the experiences by which the boy reaches a maturity or a realization of his own consciousness should be seen as representations of experiences common to the whole group. In this case the nameless and even non-individualized young character of most stories represents a Chicano generation that did not as much negate certain old traditions as it became different from the rest by effect of education and experience in a new world. The young boy is not alone in his breaking loose from the old traditions. As such, Rivera's narrative supports the hypothesis that for Latin American authors the narratives of youth are much more than sentimental recollections of a personal time when life was simpler and more magical; they are in essence the expression of a general state of maturation among emerging societies. What really counts in the intellectual and emotional experience of the Chicano is the moment of passage from one set of rules and conceptions to another one.

For Tomás Rivera this passage represents a positive step away from dependencies related to a pre-rational state akin to magic and the mystery of a sacred view of creation and humanity. As it happens with traditional, positivistic *Bildungsroman*, the religious crisis of adolescence takes a central position among the experiences which account for the growing up of the protagonist from a child to a man. The sexual awakening, in the form of a first direct or vicarious experience, is also a common factor in the narratives of growing up, and not unlikely to be seen in combination with the religious crisis. Significantly enough, both aspects are seen together in "*. . . y no se lo tragó la tierra*," and their treatment, more than their being narrated at all, provides a clue for an interpretation of how Rivera sees the outcome of the ritual of passage. For him the ritual is less a sacred ceremony than a social act. That he selects the concept of ritual to express a social encounter by which the individual finds its position in the total body of the people and its traditions is an indication of the switch he has made from a view of the world in sacred terms to the sacralization of sorts of the human will to coalesce and be one strong body. It is evident, then, that for Tomás Rivera the ritual can be found in many human activities and represents a positive function of the human mind, as it pervades all efforts directed toward the assumption of an identity, a sense of being an individual and belonging to a people. Therefore, it is not surprising to find that in his fiction Rivera makes ample use of the ritual, this time in the actual representation of the ritual act, rather than in its commenting it in analytical terms.

Several are the ritualistic actions narrated in "*. . . y no se lo tragó la tierra*"; from the most evident ones—the prayer in "Un rezo" (pp. 14-15), the spiritist seance (p. 13), the convocation of the Devil in "La noche estaba plateada" (pp. 54-56), the First Communion (pp. 82-85), for instance—to the most subtly suggested rituals of everyday life, as in the case of the poet's public readings (p. 163) or the mock boxing match in "Los quemaditos" (pp. 94-96). Ritualistic are, in a sense, the death of the lover in "La noche que se apagaron las luces" and the words of the migrant workers in "Cuando lleguemos" (pp. 148-152). Even the sequence of the several narrations, alternating with the brief texts, conform to a ritualistic structure whose both extremes are clearly designed as rituals of passage in the old tradition of the genre. In fact, as it has been observed, the summation of stories amounts to a series of steps in the process of personal maturation.[24] "*. . . y no se lo tragó la tierra*" constitutes a highly structured text that has to be read as a ritual of personal and social awareness, as a ritual celebrating humanity.

The same process of humanization seen in Rivera's interpretation of the ritual affects his understanding of religion. Devoid of any sacred value, religion and the religious forms become for him only manifestations of social and cultural traits characteristic of an old society, the one represented by the Southwest Mexican-American communities that have persisted in their own ways through years of social and cultural submission. Against the religious rituals the new Chicano poses the rituals of socialization and of self-discovery that represent a change from a state of submission to a state of self-determination. The treatment of the sacred, the ritual and the religious forms responds in Tomás Rivera to a plan for the future of his people. By pointing out in "*. . . y no se lo tragó la tierra*" the shortcomings of a religious tradition in the form of a personal subversion of those values, the author is putting in action his own ideas about the function of literature as a means for the people to invent themselves:

> Chicano literature is an attempt to give form, harmony and unity to Chicano life because as long as Chicano life exists, it manifests itself as meaningful. And thus Chicano art, literature and drama appear—in short, the Chicano creates himself and his future as a humanly total being.[25]

This attitude is what Lizárraga, following Rodríguez's ideological analysis of religion, has defined as a will for change,[26] and it is also the basis for seeing Rivera as a truly revolutionary writer. At the root of this revolutionary attitude is the educator's belief in the power of education, the liberal humanist view that appears in stark contrast with the submissive attitudes of a people used to accepting their lot as dictated by destiny.

The opposition between the old ways and the new understanding of reality embodied in the young protagonist becomes a motif in "*. . . y no se lo tragó la tierra*." The stories "offer a dynamic presentation of the protagonist who acts as the center of the action and proposes to aid his people to reach a new level of consciousness. He offers change from a deeply rooted tradition of obedience and from set laws in religion, the family, and the powerful.''[27] Thus, the words or experiences related to ''understanding'' or ''becoming aware'' of the world are common in the text, while the expressions of fear and uncertainty are also repeatedly used, in most cases in contrast to knowledge. Rodríguez del Pino has analyzed the contrasting values of the terms ''fear'' and ''anger'' in reference to a political awakening: ''el miedo como término connotativo de la opresión del pueblo y el coraje como representativo de una toma de conciencia.''[28] Another factor also affecting the attitude of the protagonist, although it is barely present in the text, could be the cynicism resulting from the loss of faith in the traditional values, as suggested by the autobiographical commentary already cited: ''By the time of high school graduation I was reading about religion and I became pretty cynical.''[29]

It is the stressing of the opposition to the set values and rules of the group, the fight between the superstitious ignorance of the old people and the new mentality of the young boy that makes in part for the much commented structure of the book. The framing of the several stories and anecdotes with two interiorized monologues expressing the personal enlightenment acquired after a sense of fear or uncertitude not only ties together the various apparently unrelated narratives, it also underlies the experience of learning, the moment of the ritual of passage from an age of faith and sacred fear corresponding both to the childhood of the protagonist and the cultural level of his people, to a mature stage of intellectual knowledge and positive reasoning corresponding to the mature intellectual age of the young character and to the cultural charactersitics of a modern, pragmatic society.

Of the two texts used as frames for the whole book, the one at the beginning, ''El año perdido'' (p. 1), introduces the basic emotive and intellectual pattern of oppositions between ignorance and knowledge. First is the idea that fear generates the desire for knowledge: ''Uña vez se detuvo antes de dar la vuelta entera y le entró miedo. Se dio cuenta de que él mismo se había llamado. Y así empezó el año perdido.'' The repetition of the expression ''darse cuenta'' three times in a text of only twenty lines stresses the function of intellectual awakening to a new understanding of the personal, and consequently collective, circumstance. The image of the ''lost year'' as the year that starts with the realization that he is the one who is calling him, searching for himself, and trying to get together with himself, can be explained in terms of the temporality of the ritual, as the ''otro tiempo (situado en un pasado mítico o en una actualidad pura).''[30] The search for himself becomes a ritual. ''Debajo de la casa'' (pp. 164-169), the internal monologue closing the frame of the work, represents also a ritualistic act. From the selection of the locale, and the position under the house, with its references to sacrifice in the biting of the fleas, to the alternation of two levels of consciousness, with the more or less objective narration of the ritual itself and the recitation almost in a trance of the several significant experiences narrated throughout the book, this text is marked by a sense of sacrality and ritual in common life.

The twelve stories, and the thirteen vignettes alternating with them, are arranged with no clear chronological order precisely because they are not supposed to represent a logical development but, instead, a series of moments that in their own intensity escape time and become a present, a paradigm. This scrambling or erasure of time is made more evident and effective at the end, when the different anecdotes are remembered by the boy in a typical stream of consciousness technique that insists in blurring any possible idea of a logical or chronological order of succession. As indicated already, the structuring of the book in this manner stresses a ritualistic reading by which the alternation of texts is interpreted as a form of liturgical rhythm suggesting subtle correspondences. In addition to this ritualized composition of the book, the individual texts directly related to a religious sense of ritual add stronger structural links to the whole in terms of themes, motifs, scenes, images and words that interact with one another.

To establish the many correspondences or coordinations between the different parts of the book would require lengthy analyses that would have to incorporate all of the critical commentaries already published. For now, and only in relation to the subject under consideration, it should be sufficient to try a brief analysis of some of the different pairs formed by a vignette and a short story. The relationship existing between these two types of texts is not always evident; it suggests the intention of creating an effect based on the contrast of the different pieces as much as on their coordination. A careful reading should be able to discern all the connections and points of contact. The intended function of this arrangement of the texts must have been, precisely, to demand from the reader an effort in active participation. It is impossible to miss the allure of the ritualistic positioning of the texts; the reader cannot but search for relationships between them, and as long as those relationships are subtle, diffuse, or obscure the normally passive act of reading will have to be transformed into a demanding search for meaningful correlations. Such exercise becomes a form of ritual participation.

The first vignette, for instance, has a subtle point of contact with the first story, "Los niños no se aguantaron" (pp. 6-7), in a common element: water. It is difficult at the beginning to see a relationship between the rather humorous situation of the boy drinking the glass of water each night that his mother left under the bed for the spirits and the tragic and violent scene of the boy killed at the water tank by a greedy farmer. Subliminally the points of contact work a pattern of understanding in which old and new values mingle and get confused. In her faithful ignorance the mother is not hurt by the plain, crude, albeit harmless, truth. She never knew ("nunca supo") that the water was not consumed by the spirits; she always believed ("siempre creyó") in supersticious dogmas. On the other hand, confronted by the tragic consequence of his greed, the farmer loses his mind and becomes less than a person. For him the breaking of a natural law, the knowledge of it, proves too damaging. In both situations the real world is seen in the act of drinking. In both cases is a child the one who drinks furtively from a forbidden source: the glass of water left for the spirits and the water for the animals. The breaking of the rule does not lead to negative consequences in the first instance because it only has to do with a world of fantasy; in the second one, the tragic and senseless consequence is the result of a brutal reality: the rules of human abuse.

No teachings or morals are advanced by the writer from these two texts. The simple juxtaposition of both anecdotes with their apparently unrelated common points works as the message at a level beyond logical understanding. Drinking, the breaking of a rule, the fear of consequences and the consequences themselves are all present in both texts. And in both texts they form a common pattern akin to a ritualistic ceremony. The killing of the boy at the water tank leads to an interpretation of a sacrificial death, while the drinking of the sacred water points to an unintentional ceremony of communion with the ancestors. But while one of the ceremonies generates for the individual knowledge and freedom from fear, the other seems senseless in its perpetuation of a cruel ritual of death. As it is, this set of texts works as a negative comment on the established social system and on the inability of the people to understand it. Together the two anecdotes communicate Rivera's central idea of the two opposing worlds: that of the traditional people who face reality from an ignorant perspective and deal with it in negative ritualistic acts of submission to the circumstances, and the world of the child who imposes a renewed ritual of knowledge and transformation. A similar interpretation should apply to the rest of the book.

The relationship between the next vignette and the subsequent story—"Un rezo" (pp. 14 15)—is more explicit. From the start they are seen as parallel rituals. A correspondence or continuity with the previous set is probably quite evident to most readers. The mother's superstitious belief in spirits is confirmed here in the search for news of the son, who has been reported lost in action in Korea, through the pagan ritual of a spiritist seance. As in the previous example, the vignette offers a rather humorous view of the situation, underlining the narrator's critical point of view. This superstitious act is clearly compared with the religious act of prayer, which, moreover, is marked by subtle references to pre-Columbian religious rites and beliefs as observed by Daniel P. Testa: "In recalling the Aztec sacrificial ritual Rivera communicates a powerful intensity in the mother's groping for understanding through such primitive beliefs."[31] The opposing view of the younger generation is missing here, except for the tacit criticism implied in the pairing of the two texts and in the relationships with the two previous ones. For Rivera criticism takes the most elusive forms in part because he cannot avoid caring for and understanding his people and his characters.

The main motif of the book appears in the fifth set of paired texts and can be seen as a natural consequence of the previous selections which have been addressing the problem of ignorance or misunderstanding of what is happening in the real world. The anecdote about the Chicano boy who is denied service at the barbershop (p. 53) pairs very well with the story of the boy who summons the devil only to conclude that there is not such a thing as a bad spirit, and that consequently there is no God either. The painful experience of realization is the common element in both texts and points to the essence of the whole book. Another coincidence is that both narratives deal with failed rituals: the tentatively Faustian summoning of the devil, and the purely socially regulated custom, and that both result in a learning process. These two selections can be seen as pointing directly to a climax within the book. Such a climax is reached in the next pair of texts, which, being the sixth pair in the book, is set almost at the center of the collection.

The religious basis of this pair has an antecedent in the previous pair and also in the first two selections, in which the direct references to the mother's belief in spirits and in the Virgin of Guadalupe have to be seen as an indication of the importance of the subject of religion which will be developed throughout the book. In the central vignette and the accompanying story—"... y no se lo tragó la tierra" (pp. 66-70)—the motif is the development or conclusion of the less than faithful attitude shown by the boy at the beginning of the book, when he drinks the water for the spirits left under the bed by his mother. In that anecdote a point of great importance is that the boy decides not to tell his mother about his action because he feels that she will not interpret the situation in the same way that he does; in other words, he senses that she will not react logically to the fact that the water was not drunk by the spirits, nor to the telling fact that her son did not suffer any bad consequences because of the sacrilegious action of drinking the forbidden water. As in that case, in the story about the boy's realization that his blasphemy does not produce any bad consequences, he decides not to tell his mother about his discovery. The schism between his worldview and that of his mother is total and represents the big gap existing between two generations of Chicanos. The humorous anecdote about the minister (p. 65) fits perfectly in this new rational, somehow cynical view of religion.

Continuing with the climactic part of the book, the next couple of texts deal with the opposition between traditional religious beliefs and the ability to understand reality. The grandfather, who gets angry at his grandson for wanting to be already thirty years old "para saber lo que había pasado con su vida," (p. 81) understands from his situation as a paralyzed old man the fascination of living, of experiencing the mystery of life. In perfect correlation to this anecdote, the experience of the boy on the day of his First Communion, narrated in the story "Primera comunión" (pp. 82-85), stresses the process of understanding the surprising experience of becoming aware of being alive. While the short anecdote ends with a direct reference to the aging process as a way of "understanding" and "becoming aware"—"El nieto no comprendió por qué le había llamado estúpido hasta que cumplió los treinta años" (p. 81)—, the short story relates the need for knowledge with the curiosity aroused by the exposure to the sexual act, and both of these with the theological concept of grace. At the end of the story the boy is in the threshold of understanding:

> Me trepé en un árbol y allí me quedé mucho rato hasta que me cansé de pensar. Cada rato recordaba la escena de la sastrería y allá solo hasta me entraba gusto al repasar. Hasta se me olvidó que le había echado mentiras al padre. Y luego me sentí lo mismo que cuando había oído hablar al misionero acerca de la gracia de Dios. Tenía ganas de saber de todo. Y luego pensé que a lo mejor era lo mismo. (p. 85)

The same scene of the boy up in the tree thinking about what he has seen reappears at the end of the book to indicate the final triumph of knowledge. It has been observed that the tree represents knowledge, as in the biblical tree of paradise.[32] The symbolic reference is quite adequate: In the first instance the key that opens the awareness of the boy is sexual knowledge; at the end, the climbing of the tree represents the awareness of his humanity and of his belonging to a world where all men are equal, no matter how far apart or unrelated they appear to be:

> Luego cuando llegó a la casa se fue al árbol que estaba en el solar. Se subió. En el horizonte encontró una palma y se imaginó que ahí estaba alguien trepado viéndolo a él. Y hasta levantó el brazo y lo movió para atrás y para adelante para que viera que él sabía que estaba allí. (p. 169)

The ritualistic aspect of climbing a tree cannot be overlooked, much less the act of waving to a distant tree. In one case the climbing is a form of personal retreat, a hiding away, as crawling under the house to think things out, or as visiting a church. In the other situation climbing becomes the first act of becoming public, of making the ritual of remembering a communal one, a true Fiesta of the living.

It should not come as a surprise, then, that the anecdote preceding the last segment of the book deals with Bartolo, the street poet whose poems were bought by the people because "en los poemas se encontraban los nombres de la gente del pueblo" (p. 164). This direct reference to the idea that literature brings people together is fully developed in the literary text to imply the same idea expressed in the essay "Chicano Literature: Fiesta of the Living:" In literature there is a form of ritual, a Fiesta in which the community of people find their common destiny. The subtle allusions to the sacred and the religious custom of public prayer add to the understanding of the brief anecdote:

> Y cuando los leía en voz alta era algo emocionante y serio. Recuerdo que una vez le dijo a la raza que leyeran los poemas en voz alta porque la voz era la semilla del amor en la oscuridad. (p. 164)

It is not a coincidence that in the same article Rivera addresses the subject of Bartolo and poetry and cites from the vignette of ". . . *y no se lo tragó la tierra.*" It was Bartolo, a true character from his boyhood years, who served as a link between the Chicano child searching for connections and the awareness of a people and their collective memory:

> Bartolo's poetry was my first contact with literature by my own people. It was to be my only contact for a long time. The bond that I felt with him and that I feel with other Chicano writers is the same.[33]

It is obvious, then, that Rivera has a clear concept of what is literature and is his mission as a writer. Unfortunately, this mission does not necessarily meet with the approval of the people. The different acts by which the young character in the stories becomes aware of a different level of reality and refuses to accept the negative aspects of his people make him different from the rest. This difference is not only an indication of generational gaps caused by the effects of Anglo society over the younger ones, but it points to the fact that this character is the poet. The coincidence with the traditional narratives of passage, the *Bildungsroman*, is another indication that Rivera is showing in this book the growth of that conscience of *la raza* embodied in the artist, the individual who can face fear and come out as a winner in the battle with old traditions. To do this he has to conquer fear and face reality. But the knowledge of truth has always had a price: madness, as when men go crazy after summoning the Devil and discovering that neither the Devil nor God have any existence:

> Pensó que bien decía la gente que no se jugaba con el diablo. Luego comprendió todo. Los que le llamaban al diablo y se volvían locos, no se volvían locos porque se les aparecía sino al contrario, porque no se les aparecía. (p. 56)

The popular misconception of madness resulting from thinking or knowing has a long tradition in history. Madness is in many cases related to poets and saints.[34] In the case of this work, madness is clearly related to such tradition as it is attached to the poet, and this one is directly related to the sacred aspect of the ritual. The young protagonist, who through thinking has reached an awareness and a knowledge not available to all of his people, is himself a poet. Thus, when he is pulled out from under the house where he has been thinking and reaching a level of wisdom superior to the one reached by his peers, the comment among the people who see him leave is quite clear:

> Pobre familia. Primero la mamá, y ahora éste. Se estará volviendo loco. Yo creo que se le está yendo la mente. Está perdiendo los años. (p. 169)

And, certainly, from the point of view of the people he always will remain a little crazy precisely because he has reached that level of understanding that they cannot reach.

The expression "perder los años" is finally understood as meaning a loss of the mind, of the common activity, of what is expected of every child. But the writer in his secluded place of meditation has been doing something that finally will affect all of his people, he has been finding and understanding everything:

> Se sintió contento de pronto porque al pensar sobre lo que había dicho la señora se dio cuenta de que en realidad no había perdido nada. Había encontrado. Encontrar y reencontrar y juntar. Relacionar esto con esto, eso con aquello, todo con todo. Eso era. Eso era todo. Y le dio más gusto. (p. 169)

Traditional religion is undercut by Rivera's appropriation of a different ritual, a ritual that is by no means new. In his early years he discovered the greatness of Whitman. That greatness was the same "serious and emotional something" that his people and even himself found in Bartolo's public readings. After his new awareness of poetic power Tomás Rivera directed all of his religious feelings, those feelings of linkage with the unknown and with the rest of men, and all his ritualistic sense, rowards the poetic experience, the experience left for poets, saints, and madmen.

UNIVERSITY OF WISCONSIN—MILWAUKEE

Notes

[1] Tomás Rivera, "Remembering, Discovery and Volition in the Literary Imaginative Process," *Atisbos: Journal of Chicano Research* (Summer 1975), p. 69. This idea of literature as "life in search of form" is constant in Rivera's critical thinking. He discusses it in "Into the Labyrinth: The Chicano in Literature," *Southwestern American Literature*, 2, 2 (Fall 1972), pp.90-91; and also in "Chicano Literature: Fiesta of the Living," in *The Identification and Analysis of Chicano Literature*. Ed. Francisco Jiménez (New York: Bilingual Press/Editorial Bilingüe, 1979), pp. 19-36.

[2] See "Into the Labyrinth . . .," passim; and Salvador Rodríguez del Pino, "Tomás Rivera y el compromiso a la vida," in *La novela chicana escrita en español* (Ypsilanti, MI: Bilingual Press/Editorial Bilingüe, 1982), pp. 7-10.

[3] "Cambio: Intento principal de '. . . y no se lo tragó la tierra.' " *Aztlán*, 7, 3 (1976), p. 420.

[4] *PCCLAS Proceedings: Changing Perspectives in Latin America*, 3 (1974), pp. 83-86.

[5] Cited by Rodríguez del Pino, *La novela chicana escrita en español*, p. 33.

[6] "Remembering . . .," p. 68.

[7] "Tomás Rivera," in *Chicano Literature. A Reference Guide*. Ed. Julio A. Martínez and Francisco A. Lomelí (Westport, Conn.: Greenwood Press, 1985), p. 343.

[8] "Remembering . . .," p. 71.

[9] "Remembering . . .," p. 77.

[10] Sisterdale, TX.: Sisterdale Press, 1973, p. 6.

[11] "Chicano Literature: Fiesta of the Living," passim.

[12] ". . . y no se lo tragó la tierra" (Berkeley, CA.: Publicaciones Quinto Sol, 1971), pp. 164-69.

[13] "The problematic in Tomás Rivera's '. . . y no se lo tragó la tierra.' " *Revista Chicano-Riqueña*, 6, 3 (1978), p. 45.

[14] *El Grito*, 2, 1 (1969), p. 61.

[15] *Chicano Literature. A Reference Guide*, p. 333.

[16] See note 1.

[17] See J. Jorge Klor de Alva, "Chicano Philosophy," in *Chicano Literature: A Reference Guide*, pp. 148-61.

[18] Octavio Paz, *El laberinto de la soledad* (México: Fondo de Cultura Económica, 1959), p. 190.

[19] "Chicano Literature: Fiesta of the Living," p. 19.

[20] "Remembering . . .," p.77.

[21] Juan Bruce Novoa, *Chicano Authors: Inquiry by Interview*. (Austin: University of Texas Press, 1980), p. 144.

[22] "Chicano Literature: Fiesta of the Living," p. 20.

[23] "Remembering . . .," p. 73.

[24] "Structural likewise is the scheme by which each experience narrated becomes in some sense a rite of passage, displaying the delicate and complex growth by which a young boy comes of age," Joseph Sommers, "Interpreting Tomás Rivera," in *Modern Chicano Writers*. Eds. Joseph Sommers and Tomás Ybarra-Frausto (Englewood Cliffs, N.J.: Prentice-Hall, 1979), p. 96. See also: Ralph F. Grajeda, "Tomás Rivera's Appropriation of the Chicano Past," in *Modern Chicano Writers*, p. 80; and Francisca Rascón, "La caracterización de los personajes femeninos en '. . . y no se lo tragó la tierra,' " in *Contemporary Chicano Fiction*. Ed. Vernon Lattin (Binghamton: Bilingual Press/Editorial Bilingüe, 1986), p. 142. In "Cambio: Intento principal . . ." Sylvia S. Lizárraga comments on the structure of the rites of passage as analyzed by Arnold van Gennep in *The Rites of Passage* (Chicago: University of Chicago Press, 1960); the relationship between such structure and the structure of ". . . y no se lo tragó la tierra" is indicative of the ritualistic value Rivera adscribed to his art.

[25] "Remembering . . .," p. 69.

[26] Lizárraga, p. 419.

[27] *Chicano Literature . . .*, p. 344.

[28] *La novela chicana . . .*, p. 17.

[29] Bruce Novoa, p. 144.

[30] Octavio Paz, *El laberinto de la soledad*, p. 45.

[31] "Narrative Technique and Human Experience in Tomás Rivera," in *Modern Chicano Writers*, p. 88.

[32] Juan Rodríguez, "Acercamiento a cuatro relatos de '. . . y no se lo tragó la tierra,' " *Mester*, 5, 1 (1974), pp. 21-23.

[33] "Chicano Literature: Fiesta of the Living," p. 20.

[34] In my article "La locura en Gabriela Mistral," *Revista Chilena de Literatura*, 21 (1983), pp. 47-62, I deal with the subject of madness in poetry and religion.

VII.   The Archive

THE TOMAS RIVERA ARCHIVE

Armando Martínez-S.

(In the Spring of 1985, the University of California, Riverside (UCR) General Library was renamed the Tomás Rivera Library by the Regents of the University of California in honor of the late Chancellor. At that time Mrs. Concepción Rivera placed her late husband's papers on loan in the library. The author serves as archivist of the Tomás Rivera Archives.)

As we know, Dr. Tomás Rivera was a multi-dimensional American educator, administrator, and writer. He provided new spectrums of creativity and vision through his leadership in education, especially at UCR. Above all, he also recognized that today's youth are our strongest national resource for carrying on American ideals.

As a national leader on Hispanic educational issues and a member of numerous foundations and boards, he was named Chancellor of UCR in July 1979. Prior to this he served as Executive Vice President at the University of Texas at El Paso and as Vice President of Administration at the University of Texas at San Antonio.

Tomás Rivera in many ways had a universal perspective which he integrated into American society. His views and value system were based on humanistic qualities, civic morality and intellectual freedom. It's clear that Rivera perceived the role of an educator/administrator as a bridge in uniting various disciplines in the arena of higher education.

An articulate speaker on the themes of higher education and Chicano literature, he emphasized Latino/Chicano creativity and presented many speeches on the educational development of Chicano scholars and their importance to the Chicano community. In an open letter to the community he stated:

> In the last analysis higher education is the last defense in civic morality. I believe this to be the greatest challenge to academe. We need to take care to ensure that our institutions of higher education provide our country with this impetus.

As is known, Tomás Rivera pursued higher education and earned Master's degrees in Education and in Spanish Literature receiving his Doctorate in 1969. As a poet and author he was among the vanguard of Chicano intellectuals arising out of the Southwest beginning in the early 1970s.

The Latino/Chicano philosophical perspective was the center of Rivera's writings. Three examples of these are:

La ideología del hombre en la obra poética de León Felipe. Dissertation, University of Oklahoma, 1969, 156 pp.

"*. . . y no se lo tragó la tierra*"/And the Earth did not Part. Berkeley, CA: Quinto Sol, 1971. 177 pp. (a novel)

Always and Other Poems. Sisterdale, TX: Sisterdale Press, 1973. 15 pp.

In time, Dr. Rivera acquired an international reputation through his writings. His work has been reviewed favorably in Europe, Latin America, Mexico, and the United States.

On February 28th, 1974, Dr. Luis Dávila, professor of Spanish and Portuguese at Indiana University, Bloomington, hosted a symposium on Chicano literature, entitled "The Chicano Short Story," featuring Tomás Rivera, Rudolfo Anaya, and Rolando Hinojosa. In many ways this colloquium chartered the future course for Chicano literature within academia. More importantly, it recognized Tomás Rivera as one of the leading catalysts in the field, and in the expression of Chicano literature, criticism, and publishing.

The importance of the Rivera Archive is firmly established by the accumulation of twenty years of material received by Dr. Rivera from colleagues, institutions, and other entities involved in the advancement of the humanities. The research potential exists chiefly in the areas of Chicano and Spanish literature, Mexican-American studies, higher education, and Administrative studies. These potential fields for research show that this archive is one of the most important Latino/Chicano collections in the State of California.

The Rivera Archive consists of approximately 75,000 items divided into four categories: the Biographical, Literary, Educational and Administrative. Currently, the archive includes original manuscripts, personal and business correspondence, illustrative materials, and over 1000 books from Dr. Rivera's private library, and we hope to add more.

The Biographical section includes manuscript compositions and printed material on the life and philosophy of Dr. Rivera, covering chiefly the years 1965 to 1984. It includes articles, photographs, awards, and audio/video tapes representing his achievements and contributions.

The Literary section consists of Dr. Rivera's original manuscripts and publications in Chicano and Spanish literature, covering chiefly the years 1970 to 1984. His unpublished poetry, and the unpublished novel *La Casa Grande,* his thesis, and drafts of published books reveal the author's literary talents. The correspondence between Dr. Rivera and other Chicano writers clearly shows the involvement and contributions Dr. Rivera made to the Chicano literary movement.

The Educational section demonstrates the contacts that Dr. Rivera maintained with the nation's leading educators, covering chiefly the years 1969 to 1984. Included are files from the organizations he participated in, and his research and teaching outlines for his courses in Chicano and Spanish literature at various universities.

Lastly, the Administrative section is composed of material from his work at the University of Texas at San Antonio (1972-78), the University of Texas at El Paso (1978-79), and the University of California, Riverside (1979-84) as an executive officer. Included are relevant papers concerning the administrative polices of these universities and Dr. Rivera's role in formulating them.

The contents of the Archive are being entered into a Database 3 Plus computer program in order to publish a catalog of its holdings by the Fall of 1987.

THE TOMAS RIVERA ARCHIVE

VIII.   The Last Song

it has been said

it has been said that when
the poet misplaces sorrow
his song is lost, the vision ceases
hunger invades, hearts b
violent force and poverty abounds
southern children smile
northern powers stalk
natural resources, birthright and sweat. theirs
if they only knew that the only gold
to b swept in the "states"
lies plastered on the streets
. . . mashed chicklets
afterall, mexican

Family picture taken at the Chancellor's residence, University of California, Riverside, 1979. Standing are Tomás and his wife, Concepción (Concha); seated, left to right, are Irasema, Javier, and Ileana.

The inauguration of Tomás Rivera as Chancellor of the University of California, Riverside, in 1980. Standing next to Tomás is the President of the University of California, David S. Saxon, and behind them (in academic cap) is Ivan Hinderaker, the retiring Chancellor.

At the inauguration at the University of California, Riverside, 1980.

Photo taken during the reception in the UCR cafeteria after the inauguration ceremony in 1980.

Tomás Rivera delivering his acceptance speech after receiving his honorary Doctor of Education degree at the University of Santa Clara, June 14, 1980. Photo by Robert H. Cox.

Portrait of the Chancellor taken in his office at the University of California, Riverside, in 1982.

Chairing the Chancellor's Executive Advisory Committee at the University of California, Riverside, 1982.

Photo of (left to right) Ron Arias, Rolando Hinojosa, Tomás Rivera, and Héctor Márquez, taken at the home of Ron Arias in Pomona, California, c. 1982, during an informal visit. Photo by Joan Arias.

IX. Bibliography

A BIBLIOGRAPHY OF WRITINGS ABOUT
TOMAS RIVERA AND HIS WORKS*

Abbot, James H. "Tomás Rivera, 1935-1984, So Proud of You Forever." *Sooner Magazine* 4.4 (1984): 21-23. Rpt. in this volume, section IV.

_____. "'. . . y no se lo tragó la tierra': With Tomás Rivera in Spain and Personal Memories." *International Studies in Honor of Tomás Rivera*. Ed. Julián Olivares. Houston: Arte Público P, 1986. 26-29.

Akers, John C. "Fragmentation in the Chicano Novel: Literary Technique and Cultural Identity." *International Studies in Honor of Tomás Rivera*. Ed. Julián Olivares. Houston: Arte Público P, 1986. 121-35.

Alurista. "Cultural Nationalism and Xicano Literature During the Decade of 1965-1975." *MELUS* 8.2 (1981): 22-34.

Blouin, Egla Morales. "Símbolos y motivos nahuas en la literatura chicana." *The Bilingual Review/La Revista Bilingüe* 5.1-2 (1978): 99-106. Rpt. in *The Identification and Analysis of Chicano Literature*. Ed. Francisco Jiménez. Jamaica, NY: Bilingual P, 1979. 179-90.

Bornstein-Somoza, Miriam. "El simbolismo como aspecto temático y estructural en 'Las salamandras' de Tomás Rivera." Unpublished ms.

Brinson-Piñeda, Bárbara. "John Steinbeck's *The Grapes of Wrath* and Tomás Rivera's '. . . y no se lo tragó la tierra': Two Visions of American Migratory Life." Unpublished ms.

Bruce-Novoa, Juan. "The Expanding Space of Chicano Literature. Update: 1978." Canto al Pueblo Convention. Corpus Christi, TX, 5 June 1978.

_____. "Literatura chicana: Una respuesta al caos." *Revista de la Universidad de México* 29.12 (1975): 20-24.

_____. "Portraits of the Chicano Artist as a Young Man. The Making of the 'Author' in Three Chicano Novels." *Festival Flor y Canto II*. Eds. Arnold C. Vento, Alurista, José Flores Peregrino, et al. Albuquerque: Pajarito Publications, 1979. 150-61.

_____. "Roundtable on Chicano Literature." *The Journal of Ethnic Studies* 3.1 (1975): 99-103.

_____. "The Space of Chicano Literature." *The Chicano Literary World 1974*. Eds. Felipe Ortego y Gasca and David Conde. Las Vegas, NM: New Mexico Highlands U, 1975. 29-58. Rpt. in *De colores* 1.4 (1975): 22-42.

_____. *Chicano Authors: Inquiry by Interview*. Austin: U of Texas P, 1980.

Campos, Jorge. "Literatura chicana: Cuentos de Tomás Rivera." *Insula* 29.328 (1974): 11.

Cárdenas de Dwyer, Carlota. "Cultural Regionalism and Chicano Literature." *Western American Literature* 15.3 (1980): 187-94.

_____. "Cultural Nationalism and Chicano Literature in the Eighties." *MELUS* 8.2 (1981): 40-47.

Carrillo, Bert. "Tomás Rivera's '. . . y no se lo tragó la tierra': Growing Up Alienated." Rocky Mountain MLA Conference. Phoenix, AZ, 27 October 1978.

Carrillo, Loretta. "The Search for Selfhood and Order in Contemporary Chicano Fiction." *DAI* 40 (1980): 4034A. Michigan State U, 1979.

---

*This bibliography was originally compiled by Tomás Rivera. Since his death, it has been updated and expanded by Juliette L. Spence (Arizona State University). It incorporates critical essays, masters' theses and doctoral dissertations, and addresses about Rivera's works, as well as recollections about Rivera himself.

Dávila, Luis. "Chicano Fantasy Through a Glass Darkly." *Otros mundos, otros fuegos; Fantasía y realismo mágico en Iberoamérica (Memoria del XVI Congreso del Instituto Internacional de Literatura Iberoamericana).* Ed. Donald A. Yates. East Lansing: Michigan State UP, 1975. 245-58.

_____. "Labyrinthic Literary Radicals: Rulfo, Paz, and Rivera." Symposium on ". . . *y no se lo tragó la tierra.*" Indiana U, 6-7 April 1972.

_____. "Otherness in Chicano Literature." *Contemporary Mexico: Papers of the Fourth International Congress of Mexican History.* Eds. James W. Wilkie, Michael C. Meyer, and Edna Monzón de Wilkie. Berkeley, CA: U of California P, 1976. 556-63.

Daydí-Tolson, Santiago. "Ritual and Religion in Tomás Rivera's Work." This volume, section VI.

Dovalina, Fernando. "Rivera: A Greek Tragedy with Chicano Actors." *Houston Chronicle* 16 January 1972: 12.

Eger, Ernestina N. "Bibliography of Works by and about Tomás Rivera." *Carta abierta* 16 (1980): 2-7.

_____. "A Selected Bibliography of Criticism of the Chicano Novel." *Contemporary Chicano Fiction: A Critical Survey.* Ed. Vernon E. Lattin. Binghamton, NY: Bilingual P, 1986. 316-31.

Elizondo, Sergio D. "Fondo y forma en la narrativa chicana." *Proceedings: IV Congreso de la Nueva Narrativa Hispanoamericana.* Calí, Colombia: Universidad del Valle, 1974. 1-10.

_____. "Myth and Reality in Chicano Literature." *Latin American Literary Review* 5.10 (1977): 23-31.

Flores, Lauro. "The Discourse of Silence in the Narrative of Tomás Rivera." *International Studies in Honor of Tomás Rivera.* Ed. Julián Olivares. Houston: Arte Público P, 1986. 96-106.

Fuente, Patricia de la. "Invisible Women in the Narrative of Tomás Rivera." *International Studies in Honor of Tomás Rivera.* Ed. Julián Olivares. Houston: Arte Público P, 1986. 81-89.

García-Girón, Edmundo. "The Chicanos: An Overview." *Ethnic Literatures Since 1776: The Many Voices of America.* Eds. Wolodymyr T. Zyla, and Wendell N. Aycock. Lubbock, TX: Texas Tech P, 1978. 87-119.

Garza, Rudolph O. de la, and Rowena Rivera. "The Socio-Political World of the Chicano: A Comparative Analysis of Social, Scientific, and Literary Perspectives." *Minority Language and Literature: Retrospective and Perspective.* Ed. Dexter Fisher. New York: MLA, 1977. 42-64.

Gonzales, Lucy. "Conflict and Struggle: A Study of Themes in the Chicano Novel." Thesis. U of Houston, 1974.

González, William H. Review of ". . . *y no se lo tragó la tierra,*" by Tomás Rivera. *Modern Language Journal* 57.4 (1973): 229.

González-Berry, Erlinda. "Chicano Literature in Spanish: Roots and Content." Diss. U of New Mexico, 1978.

_____, and Tey Diana Rebolledo. "Growing Up Chicano: Tomás Rivera and Sandra Cisneros." *International Studies in Honor of Tomás Rivera.* Ed. Julián Olivares. Houston: Arte Público P, 1986. 109-19.

Grajeda, Rafael F. "Tomás Rivera's '. . . *y no se lo tragó la tierra'*: Discovery and Appropriation of the Chicano Past." *Hispania* 62 (1979): 71-81.

_____. "Tomás Rivera's Appropriation of the Chicano Past." *Modern Language Writers.* Eds. Joseph Sommers and Tomás Ybarra-Frausto. Englewood Cliffs, NJ: Prentice-Hall, 1979. 74-85. Rpt. in *Contemporary Chicano Fiction: A Critical Survey.* Ed. Vernon E. Lattin. Binghamton, NY: Bilingual P, 1986. 113-25.

_____. "The Figure of the Pocho in Contemporary Chicano Fiction." *DAI* 35 (1975): 5402-03A.

Hancock, Joel. "The Emergence of Chicano Poetry: A Survey of Sources, Themes, and Techniques." *Arizona Quarterly* 29.1 (1973): 57-73.

Herms, Dieter. "Chicano Literature: A European Perspective." *International Studies in Honor of Tomás Rivera.* Ed. Julián Olivares. Houston: Arte Público P, 1986. 163-72.

Hinojosa [Smith], Rolando. "Tomás Rivera (1935-1984)." This volume, section III.

_____. "The Structure and Meaning of Chicano Literature." MLA Convention. Chicago, 30 December 1977.

_____. "Tomás Rivera: Remembrances of an Educator and Poet." *International Studies in Honor of Tomás Rivera.* Ed. Julián Olivares. Houston: Arte Público P, 1986. 19-23.

Irizarry, Estelle. "Los hechos y la cultura en los EE. UU." *Nivel, gaceta de cultura* (México) 31 marzo 1972: 10.

Jiménez, Francisco. "Chicano Literature: Sources and Themes." *The Bilingual Review/La Revista Bilingüe* 1.1 (1974): 4-15.

Kanellos, Nicolás. "Language and Dialog in Tomás Rivera's '. . . *y no se lo tragó la tierra*'." *International Studies in Honor of Tomás Rivera*. Ed. Julián Olivares. Houston: Arte Público P, 1986. 53-65.

_____. "Rivera's Tales of God, Sin, and the Devil." Symposium on Chicano Literature. Indiana U, 28 February-1 March 1974.

_____. "Tomás Rivera." *Magazín* 1.8 (1973): 67.

Lattin, Vernon E. "Novelistic Structure and Myth in '. . .*y no se lo tragó la tierra*.' " *The Bilingual Review/La Revista Bilingüe* 9.3 (1982): 220-26.

Leal, Luis. "Remembering Tomás Rivera." This volume, section IV.

_____. "Tomás Rivera: The Ritual of Remembering." *International Studies on Tomás Rivera*. Ed. Julián Olivares. Houston: Arte Público P, 1986. 30-38.

Lewis, Marvin A. "*Peregrinos de Aztlán* and the Emergence of the Chicano Novel." *Selected Proceedings of the Third Annual Conference on Minority Studies*. Eds. George E. Carter and James R. Parker. La Crosse, WI: Institute for Minority Studies, U of Wisconsin, 1976. 143-57.

Lizárraga, Sylvia S. "Cambio: Intento principal de '. . . *y no se lo tragó la tierra*.' " *Aztlán* 7 (1976): 419-26.

_____. "The Patriarchal Ideology in 'La noche que se apagaron las luces.' " *International Studies in Honor of Tomás Rivera*. Ed. Julián Olivares. Houston: Arte Público P, 1986. 90-95.

Lomelí, Francisco A., and Donaldo W. Urioste. *Chicano Perspectives in Literature: A Critical and Annotated Bibliography*. Albuquerque: Pajarito Publications, 1976.

López, Joe Raymond. "Religion in Selected Works of Chicano Literature." Thesis. Texas Tech U, 1975.

Lyon, Ted. "Loss of Innocence in Chicano Prose." *The Identification and Analysis of Chicano Literature*. Ed. Francisco Jiménez. Jamaica, NY: Bilingual Press, 1979. 254-62.

Maguire, John David. "Searching: When Old Dreams Find Their Youth Again." *AAHE Bulletin* n.v. (May 1985): 8, 10-14. Rpt. in this volume, Section VI.

Martínez, Eliud. "Portrait of the young Chancellor as an Artist." *At UC* [University of California] *Riverside* 4.5 (1979): 3.

_____. "Tomás Rivera: Administrator, Scholar, Poet." *Books at UC* [University of California] *Riverside* n.v. (1979): 3.

_____. "Tomás Rivera: Witness and Storyteller." *International Studies in Honor of Tomás Rivera*. Ed. Julián Olivares. Houston: Arte Público P, 1986. 39-52.

Martínez, Max. "Los mejores escritores de Aztlán." *RAYAS* 2 (1978): 3.

Meléndez Hayes, Theresa. "Process in Contemporary Chicano Poetry." MLA Convention. New York, 29 December 1978.

Melville, Margarita B. "Family Values as Reflected in Mexican American Literature." *Understanding the Chicano Experience through Literature*. Ed. Nicolás Kanellos. Houston: Center for American Studies, U of Houston, 1981. 43-53.

Menton, Seymour. Review of ". . . *y no se lo tragó la tierra*," by Tomás Rivera. *Latin American Literary Review* 1.1 (1972): 111-15.

Miller, Yvette E. "The Social Message in Chicano Fiction: Tomás Rivera's '. . . *and the earth did not part*' and Raymond Barrio's *The Plum Plum Pickers*." *Selected Proceedings of the Third Annual Conference on Minority Studies*. Eds. George E. Carter and James R. Parker. La Crosse, WI: Institute for Minority Studies, U of Wisconsin, 1976. 159-64.

Olivares, Julián. "In Honor of Tomás Rivera." *International Studies in Honor of Tomás Rivera*. Ed. Julián Olivares. Houston: Arte Público P, 1986. 7-14.

_____. "The Search for Being, Identity, and Form in the Work of Tomás Rivera." *International Studies in Honor of Tomás Rivera*. Ed. Julián Olivares. Houston: Arte Público P, 1986. 66-80.

Ortego y Gasca, Felipe de. "'. . . y no se lo tragó la tierra'/And the Earth Did Not Part: A Reading and a Reminiscence." Unpublished ms.

Paredes, Américo. "Thoughts on Tomás Rivera." International Studies in Honor of Tomás Rivera. Ed. Julián Olivares. Houston: Arte Público P, 1986. 24-25.

Paredes, Raymund A. "The Evolution of Chicano Literature." MELUS 5.2 (1978): 71-110.

Pino, Frank. "Chicano Poetry: A Popular Manifesto." Journal of Popular Culture 6 (1973): 718-30.

_____. "Hispanic Tradition in Tomás Rivera's '. . . y no se lo tragó la tierra.' " Symposium on ". . . y no se lo tragó la tierra." Indiana U, 6-7 April 1972.

_____. "La literatura chicana como microcosmo del pueblo." XVII Congreso del Instituto Internacional de Literatura Iberoamericana. 3 vols. Madrid: Ediciones Cultura Hispánica del Centro Iberoamericano de Cooperación, 1978. 3: 1561-76.

_____. "Love, Sex, and Religion in Chicano Literature." Conference on Twentieth-Century Literature. Louisville, KY, 28 February-2 March 1974.

_____. "The Outsider and 'El Otro' in Tomás Rivera's '. . . y no se lo tragó la tierra.' " Books Abroad 49 (1975): 453-58.

_____. "Realidad y fantasía en '. . .y no se lo tragó la tierra' de Tomás Rivera." Otros mundos, otros fuegos; Fantasía y realismo mágico en Iberoamérica (Memoria del XVI Congreso del Instituto Internacional de Literatura Iberoamericana). Ed. Donald A. Yates. East Lansing: Michigan State UP, 1975. 249-54.

Rainey, Marianne Pettersen. "Un estudio del anglo y del chicano en cinco novelas chicanas." Thesis. Southern Illinois U, 1976.

Ramos, Luis Arturo. " '. . . y no se lo tragó la tierra.' " Caracol. 5.5 (1979): 10-11 + .

Rascón, Francisca. "La caracterización de los personajes femeninos en '. . . y no se lo tragó la tierra.' " La Palabra 1.2 (1979): 43-50.

Rascón Garza, María Luisa. "El tema de la religión en dos novelas méxico-americanas." Thesis. Texas A & I, 1975.

Reynolds, W. Ann. "No Limits but the Sky/El cielo es el límite." This volume, Section VI.

Rivera, Tomás. "Into the Labyrinth: The Chicano in Literature." Southwestern American Literature 11.2 (1972): 90-97.

_____. "Recuerdo, Descubrimiento y voluntad." Trans. Gustavo Valadez. Atisbos 1 (1975): 66-77. Rpt. in La Raza Habla (New Mexico State U) 1.1 (1976): 13-16.

_____. "Chicano Literature: Fiesta of the Living." Books Abroad 49 (1975): 439-52.

Robinson, Cecil. "Chicano Literature." Mexico and the Hispanic Southwest in American Literature. Tucson: U of Arizona P, 1977. 308-31.

Rocard, Marcienne. "The Cycle of Chicano Experience in '. . . and the earth did not part' by Tomás Rivera." Annales de l'Université de Toulouse/Le Mirail 10.1 (1974): 141-51.

Rodríguez, Alfonso. "Time as a Structural Device in Rivera's '. . . y no se lo tragó la tierra.' " Contemporary Chicano Fiction: A Critical Survey. Ed. Vernon E. Lattin. Binghamton, NY: Bilingual P, 1986. 126-30.

_____. "Tomás Rivera: The Creation of the Chicano Experience in Fiction." This volume, section IV.

Rodríguez, Joe D. "The Chicano Novel and the North American Narrative of Survival." Denver Quarterly 16.3 (1981): 64-70.

_____. "God's Silence and the Shrill of Ethnicity in the Chicano Novel." Explorations in Ethnic Studies 4.2 (1981): 14-21.

Rodríguez, Juan. "Acercamiento a cuatro relatos de '. . . y no se lo tragó la tierra.' " Mester 5.1 (1974): 16-24.

_____. "La búsqueda de identidad en tres cuentos chicanos." Unpublished ms.

_____. "El desarrollo del cuento chicano: Del folklore al tenebroso mundo del yo." Mester 4.1 (1973): 7-12. Rpt. in Fomento literario 1.3 (1973): 19-30; and The Identification and Analysis of Chicano Literature. Ed. Francisco Jiménez. Jamaica, NY: Bilingual P, 1979. 58-67.

_____. "La embestida contra la religiosidad en '. . . y no se lo tragó la tierra.' " PCCLAS Pacific Coast Council on Latin American Studies Proceedings: Changing Perspectives in Latin America 3 (1974): 83-86.

_____. "The Problematic in Tomás Rivera's '. . . y no se lo tragó la tierra.' " *Revista Chicano-Riqueña* 6.3 (1978): 42-50.

_____. "Temas y motivos de la literatura chicana." *Festival Flor y Canto II*. Eds. Arnold C. Vento, Alurista, José Flores Peregrino, et al. Albuquerque: Pajarito Publications, 1979. 162-68.

_____. "La búsqueda de identidad y sus motivos en la literatura chicana." *The Identification and Analysis of Chicano Literature*. Ed. Francisco Jiménez. Jamaica, NY: Bilingual P, 1979. 170-78.

_____. Review of ". . . y no se lo tragó la tierra," by Tomás Rivera. *Explicación de Textos Literarios* 3.2 (1974-75): 201-02.

Rodríguez, Teresa B. "Nociones sobre el arte narrativo en '. . . y no se lo tragó la tierra.' " This volume, section VI.

Rodríguez del Pino, Salvador. "Tomás Rivera." *La novela chicana escrita en español: Cinco autores comprometidos*. Ypsilanti, MI: Bilingual P, 1982. 7-34.

Rojas, Guillermo. "La prosa chicana: Tres epígonos de la novela mexicana de la Revolución." *The Chicano Literary World 1974*. Eds. Felipe Ortego y Gasca and David Conde. Las Vegas, NM: New Mexico Highlands U, 1975. 59-70. Rpt. in *De Colores* 1.4 (1975): 43-57; *Cuadernos Americanos* (México) 34.3 (1975): 198-209; and *The Identification and Analysis of Chicano Literature*. Ed. Francisco Jiménez. Jamaica, NY: Bilingual P, 1979, 317-28.

Salazar, Verónica. "Dedication Rewarded: Prominent Mexican Americans." *The Sun* (San Antonio) 23 May 1974: n. pag.; *The San Antonio Express* 26 May 1974: n. pag.

Saldívar, Ramón. "A Dialectic of Difference: Toward a Theory of the Chicano Novel." *MELUS* 6.3 (1979): 73-92. Rpt. in *Contemporary Chicano Fiction: A Critical Survey*. Ed. Vernon E. Lattin. Binghamton, NY: Bilingual P, 1986. 13-31.

Sánchez, Federico A. "Raíces mexicanas." *Grito del Sol* 1.4 (1976): 75-87.

Sánchez, Saúl. Review of ". . . y no se lo tragó la tierra," by Tomás Rivera. *Books Abroad* 46 (1972): 633.

Santos, Alfredo G. de los, Jr. "Facing the Facts About Mexican America." This volume, Section VI.

Segade, Gustavo V. "Un panorama conceptual de la novela chicana." *Fomento literario* (Congreso Nacional de Asuntos Colegiales) 1.3 (1973): 5-18.

Sommers, Joseph. "From the Critical Premise to the Product: Critical Modes and Their Applications to a Chicano Literary Text." *New Scholar* 6 (1977): 51-80.

_____. "Interpreting Tomás Rivera." *Modern Chicano Writers*. Eds. Joseph Sommers and Tomás Ybarra-Frausto. Englewood Cliffs, NJ: Prentice-Hall, 1979. 94-107.

Somoza, Oscar U. "Grados de dependencia colectiva en '. . . y no se lo tragó la tierra.' " *La Palabra* 1.1 (1979): 40-53.

_____. "Visión axiológica en la narrativa chicana." *DAI* 38 (1978): 4203A.

Sotomayor, Frank. "An Explosion of Chicano Literary Merit." *Los Angeles Times Calendar* 28 January 1973: n. pag.

Tatum, Charles M. "Contemporary Chicano Prose Fiction: Its Ties to Mexican Literature." *Books Abroad* 49 (1975): 431-38. Rpt. in *The Identification and Analysis of Chicano Literature*. Ed. Francisco Jiménez. Jamaica, NY: Bilingual P, 1979. 47-57.

_____. *A Selected and Annotated Bibliography of Chicano Studies*. 2nd ed. Lincoln, NE: Society of Spanish and Spanish-American Studies, U of Nebraska, 1979.

_____. *Chicano Literature*. Boston: Twayne, 1982.

Testa, Daniel P. "Narrative Technique and Human Experience in Tomás Rivera." *Modern Chicano Writers*. Eds. Joseph Sommers and Tomás Ybarra-Frausto. Englewood Cliffs, NJ: Prentice-Hall, 1979. 86-93.

Thomas, George Aaron. "Tres etapas en el desarrollo de la novela chicana contemporánea." *DAI* 43 (1982): 1987A.

Valdés Fallis, Guadalupe. "Metaphysical Anxiety and the Existence of God in Contemporary Chicano Fiction." *Revista Chicano-Riqueña* 3.2 (1975): 26-33.

Vallejos, Tomás. "The Vitality of Ancient Myth and Ritual in Chicano Literature: Tomás Rivera's 'Las Salamandras.' " Midwest Foco of National Association of Chicano Studies. Notre Dame, 10 November 1979.

_____. "Mestizaje: The Transformations of Ancient Indian Religious Thought in Contemporary Chicano Fiction." *DAI* 41 (1980): 1602A.

Vásquez-Castro, Javier. *Acerca de literatura (Diálogo con tres autores chicanos)*. San Antonio, TX: M & A Editions, 1979. 39-53.

Veiga, Gustavo da. "Tomás Rivera e la literatura chicana dos Estados Unidos." *Minas Gerais Suplemento Literario* 27 May 1972: 11.

Vélez, Diana. "The Reality of the Chicanos." *The Bilingual Review/La Revista Bilingüe* 2.1-2 (1975): 203-07.

Vento, Arnold C. "Exponentes recientes de la literatura chicana en lengua hispánica." MLA Convention. Chicago, 28 December 1977; Canto al Pueblo Convention. Corpus Christi, TX, 5 June 1978.

Whitmore, Don. Review of ". . . *y no se lo tragó la tierra,*" by Tomás Rivera. *South Central MLA Bulletin* 33.3 (1973): 160-61.

Willey, Michael Lee. "The Debt to Minority Literature: Images of Change and Action in Recent White Literature." *DAI* 34 (1974): 7792-93A.

Woods, Richard D. "Self-Portraiture as Exemplified in Works of Three Quinto Sol Award Recipients: Rivera, Anaya, and Hinojosa-Smith." American Studies Association Convention. San Antonio, TX, 7 November 1975.

Zendejas, Francisco. "Multilibros." *Excelsior* 28 October 1972: 19A.